SOPHOCLES
ANTIGONE

SOPHOCLES
ANTIGONE

EDWARD ALEXANDER

INVICTUS PUBLISHING

Published in 2023 by Invictus Publishing.

© Matthew Edward Alexander Pedrick. All rights reserved.

No part of this work may be reproduced commercially without the express permission of the publisher.

Reverse cover art: "Antigone" by Félix Resurrección Hidalgo

ISBN: 9781068416309

CONTENTS

Prologue: The Curse of Oedipus	4
Antigone	10
Family and Fatherland	98
Ἀντιγόνη	148
Genealogy of the Royal House of Thebes	218
Glossary	220

"Seek ever to stand in the hard Sophoclean light
and take your wounds from it gladly"

– Ezra Pound, *Ité*

PROLOGUE

THE CURSE OF OEDIPUS

Upon the birth of his first child, King Laius of Thebes sought counsel from the Delphic oracle, who foretold that he was doomed to perish at the hands of his own son. Laius consequently had the boy's feet bound with metal pins and ordered his wife, Jocasta, to kill the child. Unable to carry out the deed herself, she instructed a servant to expose the infant upon Mount Cithæron. Out of pity, he was instead handed over in secret to a Corinthian shepherd who named the child "Oedipus" in reference to his swollen feet. The infant was taken back to Corinth and presented to the childless King Polybus and his wife Merope, who adopted the boy and raised him as their own.

Many years later, after he had reached manhood, Oedipus encountered a drunken guest during a feast who taunted him for not truly being the son of Polybus. Concerned by the man's words, he at once travelled to Delphi to speak with the oracle, only to be told that he was fated to slay his father and wed his mother. Horrified, Oedipus resolved never to return to Corinth and instead set off eastward on foot. At a narrow pass where three branching roads met, he came across an old man and his company on a wagon. A quarrel soon broke out in which Oedipus, coming under attack, defended himself, slaying both the man and his attendants. Unbeknownst to him, the old man whose life he had taken was in fact his father, Laius, the King of Thebes.

Oedipus continued on his way and in time arrived at Thebes, whose people were suffering under the torment of the Sphinx, a winged creature with the body of a lioness and the head of a human woman. Perched upon a hill, the wicked beast made sport of challenging Thebans and other passers-by to solve her riddle, and when each duly failed, she would devour them. The city had offered a tremendous reward to any who could liberate them from the Sphinx – the throne of Thebes and the hand of the widowed Queen, Jocasta, in marriage. The riddle in question went as follows: "what goes on four feet, three feet, and two feet, yet is most feeble when it walks on four?" Oedipus, accepting the challenge, answered: "man – he crawls on all fours as a baby, walks on two feet in maturity, and upon three as an old man with his stick". Bested, the Sphinx promptly threw herself from the rocks to her death, leaving Oedipus to enter the city as its liberator. He was thus made King of Thebes and took Jocasta for his wife, unaware that the woman to whom he was now married was in fact his mother.

Many years passed, during which Oedipus ruled as a beloved and prosperous king. Jocasta bore him two fine sons, Eteocles and Polynikes, along with two fair daughters, Antigone and Ismene. One day, however, a foul plague befell Thebes: a blight struck the fruits of the earth and pestilence devastated the city. According to the oracle at Delphi, the calamity would not end until the murderer of Laius was discovered and punished with either death or exile. Oedipus therefore vowed to identify and punish whoever was responsible, proclaiming a solemn curse upon the unknown offender.

In his efforts to save Thebes from the ongoing plague, Oedipus enlisted the help of the blind seer, Tiresias, who admitted to knowing the information the king sought, yet refused to speak it. After a bitter argument between the two, Tiresias revealed that the murderer was Oedipus himself. The revelation was at first rejected, but when Jocasta's attempt to console her husband spurred further questioning, Oedipus uncovered the truth of his own identity and how the terrible prophecy told to him long ago had come to pass. Jocasta immediately hanged herself in her bedchamber, and upon discovering her body, Oedipus removed the long gold pins from her robe and gouged out both his eyes.

Oedipus remained in Thebes for some years, the rule of the city being overseen by his brother-in-law, Creon, and his two young sons. Finally, at the urging of Creon, unopposed by Eteocles and Polynikes, Oedipus was sentenced to exile. Before leaving, the disgraced king cursed his two sons to die by one another's hand for having abandoned him. With his daughter Antigone as his sole companion and guide, he left the city to wander the roads of Hellas. He would eventually pass away in the town of Colonus, near Athens.

After the exiling of Oedipus, his two sons fell into quarrelling over the kingship. Eteocles seized the throne, while Polynikes was driven from the city. The aggrieved older brother fled to Argos where he married the daughter of King Adrastus. With the Argive king's support, Polynikes raised an army and marched against Thebes in order to depose Eteocles and claim the throne. At six of the city's seven gates, the Theban champion defeated his Argive adversary, while at the seventh, the two brothers met in battle and killed one another, fulfilling the curse of their father.

ANTIGONE

DRAMATIS PERSONÆ

ANTIGONE
daughter of Oedipus and Jocasta

ISMENE
sister of Antigone

CHORUS
of Theban elders

CREON
uncle of Antigone and king of Thebes

A GUARD
on sentry duty for Polynikes' corpse

HAEMON
son of Creon and Eurydice

TIRESIAS
a blind seer of renown

A MESSENGER
attendant of Creon

EURYDICE
wife of Creon and mother of Haemon

SCENE: *Night-time, in front of the royal house of Thebes. The invading Argive forces have just withdrawn from the city, abandoning their doomed campaign and the bodies of their fallen warriors. Polynikes and Eteocles, the two brothers fighting on opposing sides, have slain one another, leaving Creon, their uncle, to assume the kingship.*

Enter ANTIGONE, *followed by* ISMENE, *slipping out quietly through the main doors of the royal house.*

ANTIGONE:
O Ismene, dear sister, blood of my blood,
of all the ills passed down from our father,
is there a single one, just one I ask,
that Zeus will spare us while yet we live?
For there is nothing – no pain, no ruin,
no private shame or public dishonour,
nothing I have not seen in your woes
and mine. And now, what fresh grief is this?
A new edict, they say, decreed by the general
to all the citizens of Thebes? 10
Do you know anything? Have you not heard
that the wretched fate of enemies
now marches on the ones we love most?

ISMENE:

Not a word, Antigone, have I heard of this,
no talk of loved ones, pleasing or painful,
has come to me since that bitter blow,
the two of us, robbed, of two brothers,
each finding his death at the hand of the other.
Since the men of Argos withdrew, vanished
this very night, no more have I heard, 20
nothing of whether joy or ruin awaits us.

ANTIGONE:

I thought as much, and so I brought you here,
beyond the gates, where you alone might hear.

ISMENE:

Hear what? Trouble – that much is clear,
your words spell grief, so grave do you seem.

ANTIGONE:

How else could it be? Our brothers, our kin!
Has Creon not honoured one with all rites,
dishonoured the other? Eteocles, they say,
has been laid to rest, covered with earth
as is right, as is just, to be held in honour 30
among the dead below. Yet as for the body
of Polynikes, his misery abiding in death,
an order has come down to all the city

that none may bury or even mourn him.
He is to be left, they say, unwept, unburied,
a bountiful treasure for the circling birds
to feast upon with gluttonous joy.
Such is the law that our good king Creon
decrees for you and me – for me, Ismene!
He is coming, I hear, to inform the uninformed, 40
to make clear to each that this matter is one
he does not treat lightly. Whoever should dare
to defy this order, their fate is sealed –
death by stoning inside the public square.
This is how it stands. Soon you will show
if noble you are and worthy of your blood,
or craven, a coward, the lowest of high-born.

ISMENE:

Poor sister – if things have truly come to this,
who am I to unbind or tighten this knot,
what good can I do?

ANTIGONE:

                        That is for you to decide. 50
Will you help me, will you share the labour?

ISMENE:
What labour? What is it you intend to do?

ANTIGONE:
Will your hands help mine to lift up his body?

ISMENE:
What? You mean you would seek to bury him?
When the city has been forbidden by law?

ANTIGONE:
Yes, I do! He is my brother – and yours too,
even if you wish it were not so.
I will not forsake my duty to him;
never will it be said that I betrayed my kin.

ISMENE:
So reckless – when Creon, the king himself   60
expressly forbids it?

ANTIGONE:
             No! Enough!
He has no right to keep me from my own.

ISMENE:
O sister, please, you must take care –
think of how our father fell into ruin,
despised, detested, infamous to all,
driven by the crimes he exposed himself
to gouge out his eyes in self-blinding shame.

Then mother, his mother-wife, two yet one,
her life brought to an end in the twisted noose.
Finally, two brothers dead in a single day, 70
each slain in battle at the hand of the other,
shared doom for shared blood, a wretched fate.
And now the two us, we alone remain.
Think of how dreadful our deaths would be,
what misery it would invite if we defied the law,
disdained his authority, the power of the throne.
Remember that we are women, and as nature
decreed, it is not for us to contend with men.
Far greater is the strength of those who rule;
a might, enthroned, to which we must submit 80
in this and much worse, no matter the hardship.
I, for my part, shall ask the forgiveness
of those beneath the earth, to judge that I act
only as I must – forced, no choice but to obey
the ones in power. All else is madness;
no sense in a deed that can never be done.

ANTIGONE:

So be it. I won't insist, yet nor if your heart
should come to change will I welcome your help;
your hands, if willing, will not labour with mine.
Do as you see best – I shall bury him myself, 90
and if death follows, that death will be an honour.
I shall rest beside him, two bound by love,

a criminal sacred to the gods!
                            Far greater
is the time to please the dead than the living,
for we dwell in the world below forever.
But do as you wish – dishonour the laws
which the eternal gods hold in honour.

ISMENE:
Dishonour them I do not, yet nor have I the strength
to defy the city, to oppose the will of the king.

ANTIGONE:
Comfort yourself with excuses if you must,   100
but no longer will I stay. I am going now
to raise a grave-mound over the brother I love.

                     ANTIGONE *turns to leave.*

ISMENE:
O sister, please, you go too far – I fear for you!

ANTIGONE:
Fear not for me; think first of your own fate.

ISMENE:
Then at the very least speak nothing of this deed;
keep it hidden, a secret, and I will do the same.

ANTIGONE:
O by the gods – shout it from the city walls!
Far more will I hate you for holding your tongue,
for silence, than for proclaiming this to one and all.

ISMENE:
Such a burning rage – when it should chill your heart.   110

ANTIGONE:
I know that I please those who matter most.

ISMENE:
If you prevail, yes, but you crave the impossible.

ANTIGONE:
If that is so, then when my strength fails me,
I shall rest at last.

ISMENE:
                But you start without hope;
You grasp at a vision that can never be caught.

ANTIGONE:
If you truly mean what you say, my hatred
you will have, and the judgement of the dead.
But leave me to my folly, leave me to suffer
this dreadful thing – for I will suffer nothing,
nothing so shameful as death without honour.   120

Exit ANTIGONE *on the road leading
out beyond the city walls, towards the battlefield.*

ISMENE:
Then go, if go you must, but please know this:
however reckless your path, to the ones who love you,
you are – and always will be – truly dear.

Exit ISMENE, *withdrawing into the royal house.*

Enter the CHORUS *of Theban elders,
counsellors of the king, singing as the sun begins to rise.*

CHORUS:
*Glory be to the Sun's first rays, brightest of all
that ever dawned on the seven gates of Thebes!
At last you shine forth, great eye of golden day,
burning away darkness, the veil of shrouding night
and gliding over Dirce's battle-weary stream,
goading the men from Argos, all clad in bronze,
the white-shielded warriors in headlong retreat,
driven back, fleeing from your keen spears of rose.*

They had set out against us, our city, our land,
spurred forth by the warring claims of Polynikes;
like a shrieking eagle they swooped down upon us,
keen talons braced behind wings white as snow,
a host of crested helmets bristling for blood.
The foe hovered high above our homes, circling,
his ravenous maw gaping over the seven gates,
his spears thirsting for the wine of deep wounds.
But before his vast jaws were glutted with our gore,   140
before Hephæstus' pine-fed flames could claim
our crown of towers – he was gone.
His rival, the Dragon, he strove to subdue,
a conquest beyond him, the clash of our arms
like thunder at his back, roaring all around him.

For above all Zeus loathes the hollow bluster
of a boastful tongue. Thus when he saw them
surge forward in a rolling flood, a wave of gold
ringing and resounding with undue pride,
he brandished his lightning, hurled the fire down,   150
smiting one who had made for the highest tower,
a warrior rushing to declare their victory
from the moment he reached our walls.

*Back he fell, plummeting from the heights, down
upon the hard earth, a blazing torch
still clutched in his hand – a man possessed
just moments before by the frenzy of battle,
a tempest, raging in his fury against us.
Yet his threats did not herald the triumph he'd hoped
for the unmerciful war-god dispensed to each,* 160
*those men of Argos, his doom with savage blows – Ares,
mighty Lord of Arms, our ally at the fateful hour.*

*Seven captains stationed at seven gates,
set against seven worthy contenders,
their brazen trophies offered up to Zeus,
he who turns battles and puts foes to flight;
all save for two: that accursed pair, born
of one father, one mother, on opposing sides,
two rivals matched with twin slaying spears,
sharing in the spoils of a common death.* 170

*But now for Victory and her glorious name!
May we each exult in the blossoms of triumph
as she wings her way to rejoice with Thebes,
guiding a great host of chariots in her flight!
Let us purge the spectre of war from our minds
and gather together at the temples of the gods,
dancing, singing until the night burns away!
And may joyful Dionysus, Lord of Festivity
who shakes the land of Thebes, lead us now!*

Enter CREON *with attendants.*

But look, here comes the new king, Creon, 180
son of Menœcus – a new ruler for a new day,
for whatever the gods may have set before us.
What plan does he propose to put in motion
for which he has called this special council,
an assembly of elders all summoned at once?

CREON:
Good men of Thebes! Our ship of state is safe at last.
Long was she tossed upon the billowing waves,
rocked by a storm that nearly pulled her under,
but the gods have guided her aright once more.
I have called you here, you few alone, 190
for well I know that you have always honoured
and steadfastly served the throne of Laius.
How when Oedipus came to restore our city
your loyalty held; and when he came to ruin,
unwavering still, you stood by his children.
But now, in one day, doom's double blow –
both sons dead, each striking, each struck,
two brothers stained with the blood of the other.
By virtue of kinship with those who have passed,
the power of the throne is by right now mine. 200
It is impossible, of course, to know a man truly,
his character, his mind, his sense of judgement,
till he has proved himself in the task of ruling,

his command of the law – the test of kingship.
My view is that he who assumes the role
of governing the city, of directing its course,
yet fails to act upon the wisest counsel,
holding his tongue out of fear instead –
he is and will always be a worthless coward.
While any man who would place a friend
above the good of his own fatherland,
that man, I say, is beneath regard.
May Zeus be my witness, he who sees all, always:
never would I stand idly by if ruin I saw
marching upon the people, their safety in doubt;
nor would I ever make a friend of one
who threatened to bring our country low.
For this I know well: the city is our home,
our deliverance, our prosperity,
and only when she sails straight and true
may the bonds of real brotherhood be formed.
Such are the virtues which strengthen a city.
With these in mind I have just now proclaimed
an edict to the citizens, a law concerning
the sons of Oedipus. Eteocles, first,
who perished fighting in defence of Thebes,
excelling all in battle. He shall be buried as befits
the glory of his deeds, entombed with all honours,
every sweet libation we pour upon the earth,
descending to the noble dead below.

But as for the other, of Polynikes I speak,
who from exile returned to the home of his fathers
and the gods of his people, desiring above all
with a most violent passion to burn the city
from temple to hearth, to feast upon the blood
of his fellow kinsmen, and lead the rest into slavery –
a law has been decreed that no one in the city
may mourn him, nor dignify him with burial.
He must lie unburied, his body exposed,
carrion for the dogs and birds to tear at,   240
a fate most shameful for all to behold.
Such is my will – for never under my rule
will the traitor be honoured as befits the good.
But those who are loyal and wish the city well,
I shall honour them dearly in death as in life.

CHORUS:
If this is how you wish, son of Menœcus,
to treat the foes and friends of our city
then the power is yours, to enforce it by law
for the dead as much as for the living.

CREON:
Uphold my commands, then, and ensure they are kept.   250

CHORUS:
Younger shoulders would bear that burden better.

CREON:
That is not what I meant, not what I ask of you;
guards have already been assigned to the body.

CHORUS:
Then what is it you would command of us?

CREON:
That you never yield to, nor ally yourself with
those who would oppose me and defy my orders.

CHORUS:
There is no one so foolish as to covet death.

CREON:
Death, indeed, would be the price. Yet often
the mere hope of profit will lead men to ruin.

Enter GUARD.

GUARD:
My king, I cannot say that I arrive here breathless,   260
spent from having run, hastening with swift feet.
Far from it, in truth, for often did my thoughts
stop me in my tracks, wheeling me around,
knowing not whether to hurry or turn back.
To and fro my mind wavered, one voice saying,

"think, you fool – why go to where you know
only punishment awaits?"
                              And the other retorting,
"O witless clod, are you dallying again?
If Creon should learn of this from someone else,
would a terrible end not surely befall you?"   270
Weighing these thoughts, I tarried and trudged,
till soon the short road became impossibly long.
But at last, as is plain, the view won out
that I had best – I must – make my way here to you;
and even if my words should avail me nothing,
I will share them all the same, speak of what I know,
for I have come grasping one solitary hope:
I shall suffer nothing save that which is fated,
and my fate will unravel as fate ever must.

CREON:
What on earth is the matter? Why so fearful?   280

GUARD:
First, if I may, I must speak for myself.
I neither did this deed, nor saw who did; I only ask,
as is just, that I not be burdened with the blame.

CREON:
So desperate you are to set up your defence,
seeking distance between yourself and the deed.
It is clear you have something important to tell.

GUARD:
Terrible, in truth – enough to make one delay.

CREON:
Then speak, be free of it, and take your leave.

GUARD:
Very well. Here it is. The body –
someone has just buried it then vanished,   290
carefully sprinkled dry dust over the flesh
and attended to the proper rites.

CREON:
What are you saying? What man would dare?

GUARD:
That I do not know. There was no mark from a spade
or pick-axe to be seen, no earth turned up;
the ground, hard and dry, seemed undisturbed,
no sign of tracks, no ruts from a wheel – nothing.
Whoever did this left no trace at all.
When the first of the day-guard showed it to us,
we were stunned, silent, at a loss to understand.   300
The body was hidden – not buried
under a mound, but veiled with dust,
a light cover, as if cast by the hands of one
who could not bear to see the dead dishonoured.
There was no sign at all that dogs or wild beasts

had torn at the skin, even approached the body.
At this a great clamour arose on all sides: bitter words
flew back and forth, guard accusing guard,
every man for himself, every man the culprit,
and no one to stop it from coming to blows. 310
Yet among us not one was stained with guilt,
no proof to bear. Each pleaded his innocence,
each ready to grasp red-hot iron in his hands,
to walk through fire, swear oaths to the gods
just to clear his name, to prove he had no part in it,
no knowledge of the deed, or the one who did it.
Then, after all our efforts had come to naught,
one man spoke up and made each hang his head,
our eyes fixed in fear upon the unmarked ground.
We had no answer, no counter to his words, 320
yet neither could we envision it ending well.
For he said that the deed could not be hidden,
that it would have to be reported to you.
This view won the day, and I the prize,
condemned by lot and ill-fortune as ever.
So here I am, as unwilling, no doubt,
as I am unwelcome. For well I know
that no man cherishes the bearer of bad news.

CHORUS:
My king, I have been wondering for a while now
if this deed might somehow be the work of the gods? 330

CREON:
Enough, lest your words enrage me further,
or show you to be fools in your old age.
It is absurd – egregious – to suggest that the gods
would have the slightest concern for that corpse!
Tell me, was it in honour of his noble deeds,
his piety, that they sought to bury him? The exile
who returned to burn their pillared temples,
to set their sacred shrines aflame, to reduce
their hallowed land to ash, and scatter its laws
to the winds? Do you truly believe that the gods   340
would hold such a man in high regard? That they
would honour such treachery? Unthinkable!
No, from the very first there were certain men,
a rebellious few who could not bear to see me king,
grumbling and shaking their heads in secret,
disdainful of the law – malcontents
unwilling to bow and submit to my rule.
These men, I am convinced – it was they who led
my guards astray, bribed them to commit this deed.
For of all things, there is nothing worse for man,   350
more poisonous in our lives, than money.
It ravages cities, uproots men from their homes;
it darkens good hearts and warps honest minds,
setting them upon the most shameful of deeds;
it teaches men to hone every kind of villainy,
every crime, every impiety – money!

But whoever took the bribe may be sure of one thing:
for this deed, in time, they shall pay the penalty.

Turning to the GUARD.

By Zeus, whom I honour and hold in reverence,
I swear a solemn oath: if you do not find him, 360
the very one who buried that corpse
and bring him before me – Hades alone,
no mere death, shall be punishment enough.
You will be left to hang, alive, if only just,
until the truth of this outrage is brought to light.
Thereafter you may thieve with greater judgement,
informed of where to seek your beloved wealth,
and armed with the knowledge that it does not pay
to grasp at the fruits of each and every tree.
For more men are ruined by ill-gotten gains 370
than rewarded with long and prosperous lives.

GUARD:
May I speak, my king, or must I turn and go?

CREON:
Do you not see how maddening I find your words?

GUARD:
Which grieves you most: your ears, or your heart?

CREON:
And who are you to question my displeasure?

GUARD:
I may offend your ears, but the doer of this deed,
it is he who pains your heart.

CREON:
                              By the gods...
How plain it is that you were born to prattle.

GUARD:
Maybe so, but I did not bury that body.

CREON:
Yes you did – and what's more, you sold your life   380
for a few pieces of silver.

GUARD:
                              Ah! How terrible it is
when the one who judges misjudges all things.

CREON:
Quibble over judgement all you wish – just know
that if you fail to bring forth the offenders,
you shall soon come to swear upon the gods
that tainted money only ever brings woe.

Exit CREON *into the royal house.*

GUARD:
I pray he is found – what mercy that would be!
But whether caught or not, as fortune will decide,
I'm never coming back, you won't see me here again.
For now, somehow, beyond hope or belief, I'm saved.   390
Dear gods – I owe you my everlasting thanks!

Exit GUARD, *departing hurriedly.*

CHORUS:
Many are the wonders of this world,
yet none more remarkable than man.
This wonder traverses the surging waves,
across the heaving swell, over Poseidon's grey,
surf-crested peaks, buffeted by the bitter blades
of winter's wrath, steering his course ever onward.
Earth – the oldest of the gods, the imperishable,
the inexhaustible – he works to his own ends,
turning up the soil with plough and mule,   400
sowing and harvesting, year after year.

The lightsome, nimble birds, the wild beasts,
and the swarming sea-life that dwells in the deep,
he snares them all in the mesh of his woven nets –
man the ingenious, the cunning, the skilled!
He conquers by his craft the headstrong prey

that roams far and wide over fields and hills,
taming the stallion, binding fast his shaggy mane,
and mastering the tireless mountain bull.

Speechcraft, thought as swift as the wind, 410
and a temper disposed towards the public good –
he has trained these well; how to guard himself
from the arrows of frost, shelter from the grim,
biting cold, and the bolts of hammering rain.
Ever-inventive, ever-striving, he marches on,
prepared for whatever may come – only Death,
for all the hardships he has overcome,
from Death alone will he find no escape.

Master of invention, he forges ahead,
at once to betterment, at another to ruin. 420
When he honours the laws of the land
and the justice of the gods, as bound by oath,
both he and his city shall prosper.
Yet banished from the city, an exile is he
who courts disgrace, ignoble in his deeds
and neglectful of the good. A man such as this
will never share my thoughts, nor my hearth.

>Enter the GUARD, leading ANTIGONE.

What divine intervention is this? A sign?
But wait, do my eyes deceive me – I know her,

no use in denying it, that girl is Antigone! 430
O ill-fated child of an ill-fated father.
What could this mean? Why are you led here
like a common prisoner, a captive of the guard?
Surely you did not break the laws of the king,
caught in some mindless act of defiance?

GUARD:
Here she is, the guilty party – we found her
burying the body. And Creon, where is he?

Enter CREON *from the royal house.*

CHORUS:
Here he comes now, just when he is needed.

CREON:
Needed for what? What has happened?

GUARD:
                        My king,
there is nothing a man can swear he'll never do, 440
for second thoughts make liars of us all.
I vowed to myself that I would stay far away,
troubled as I was by your tempest of threats.
But this gift from the gods exceeded all hopes,
a joy heaven-sent beyond match or measure.
So here I am, though I swore not to return,

leading this girl, the offender you sought,
caught in the act of attending to the dead.
No casting of lots this time – this luck is mine,
my fortune alone. And now, my lord, 450
she is yours to take, to question as you wish,
to pass judgement upon. I only ask, as is right,
that I be set free, relieved of this whole ordeal.

CREON:
This girl? Where? How did you come upon her?

GUARD:
Burying the man. You know all there is to tell.

CREON:
And you speak the truth – you're certain of that?

GUARD:
I saw her burying the body with my own eyes,
the very deed you had expressly forbidden.
Surely that is clear enough, as plain as can be?

CREON:
What exactly did you see? How was she caught? 460

GUARD:
What happened was this: we returned to our post,
those grim threats of yours hanging over our heads,

and swept away the dust that cloaked the body,
leaving it uncovered and damp with decay.
Then we stationed ourselves upon the high ground,
backs to the wind so the stench could not strike us,
each man working to keep the other alert –
nudging, goading, harsh words flying back and forth,
a rollicking for anyone who dared to nod off.
And so the hours passed by until the flaming sun   470
bestrode the noon sky, a blazing disc, its heat
beating down upon us – then suddenly it happened,
a whirlwind, from nowhere, raising a great storm
of dust from the earth, a calamity of the heavens
filling the plain, tearing the leaves from every tree,
choking the air around us and shrouding the sky.
We closed our eyes, hunched our shoulders,
and endured that beating from the gods.
After a while, when the storm at last cleared,
we looked out once more – and there she was, the girl!   480
She cried out, pained, a sharp, anguished cry
like a mother bird who returns to her nest,
peering inside to find the hatchlings gone.
So it was when she saw the corpse bare,
her grief overwhelming, weeping terribly
and calling down curses upon those to blame.
Hurriedly she scooped up the parched dust
with her hands, and lifting high a fine bronze urn,
honoured the dead with three libations.
Forward we flew as soon as we saw her, closed   490

like hunters on their prey, yet she did not panic.
We questioned her, accused her of crimes
both past and present, yet she denied nothing,
owned up to it all. It's a curious thing, truly,
to find oneself torn between relief and regret.
For escaping one's troubles is a joy unmatched,
but leading a friend to ruin is pain just as pure.
So when it came to my own safety, I must confess,
I made the choice I made, I put myself first.

> CREON *fixes his gaze upon* ANTIGONE.

CREON:
And you, with your head bent towards the ground, 500
what have you to say? Do you admit you did this,
or do you deny it?

ANTIGONE:
                    I admit it. I do not deny a thing.

CREON: *(to the* GUARD*)*
You may take yourself wherever you please,
a free man once more, cleared of a grievous charge.

> *As he leaves,* CREON *turns back to* ANTIGONE.

As for you, tell me – in short, no drawn out speech –
did you know that an edict had forbidden this?

ANTIGONE:
I knew. How could I not? It was known to all.

CREON:
And still you dared to disregard the law?

ANTIGONE:
Of course – for it was not Zeus who decreed it,
the Father of All did not command this of me;   510
nor did hallowed Justice, dwelling amongst the gods
beneath the earth, ordain such laws for man;
nor did I believe your word held such force
that you, a mortal, could overrule the gods,
the unwritten and unfailing, immutable laws.
For their life is not merely of this day or the last,
but for all time, a tradition rooted in the dawn,
and no one knows when they first saw light.
Not for fear of any man, not the pride of a king,
was I prepared to break these eternal laws   520
and suffer the judgement of the gods.
Die I must, I know that well – how could I not?
As true without as with your proclamations.
And if I am to die before my time, so be it,
I shall count it a blessing. For how could anyone
who lives as I do, amidst so much misery,
not look upon death as a merciful reward?
I do not dread that fate; a painless price
would it be to pay. But if I had suffered

my mother's son, my own flesh and blood, 530
to be dishonoured in death, to lie unburied,
what torment that would have brought!
This – this is no agony. This grieves me nothing.
And if it seems to you that my actions are foolish,
then perhaps it is a fool who accuses me of folly.

CHORUS:
Like father, like daughter, an unruly child.
She has not learned to bend before trouble.

CREON:
Must I remind you that the stubborn and wilful
tend to fall the hardest; that the toughest iron,
tempered thoroughly in the swordsmith's fire, 540
will often be the first to yield and shatter.
I have seen even the wildest, most spirited horses
tamed by the smallest bit. For in those who serve,
pride endures not when their master is before them.
This girl was already well-versed in outrage
when she brazenly defied the public edicts.
But now this, the insolence, a second affront,
mocking us openly by exulting in her deed.
I am no man, not now. If she takes this victory
and leaves unpunished, she, not I, will be the man. 550
Never! Whether she is the child of my sister
or closer in blood than all who gather
to worship great Zeus at the altar of my home,

neither she nor her sister will escape their fate –
a just, dreadful end. Both, yes, for I charge the other
with an equal hand in plotting this burial.

To his attendants.

Summon her at once! I saw her just now inside,
raving, hysterical – completely gone to pieces.
As so often happens, the miscreant's mind,
plagued by guilt, convicts itself in anticipation. 560
Though far more, in truth, do I despise the traitor
who when caught seeks to glorify his crimes.

ANTIGONE:
I have been captured, caught in the act –
what more do you want than my execution?

CREON:
Nothing. With that, I shall have everything.

ANTIGONE:
Then why delay? Your lecturing is pointless;
every word repels me, and ever will it be thus,
just as all that I speak must be odious to you.
Yet what greater glory could I have gained
than by giving my own brother a burial? 570
Everyone here, they would all agree, rejoice,
were their tongues not shackled by fear.

But alas, not all have the liberty, the power
of absolute rule, to do and say as one wishes.

CREON:
You alone, of all these Thebans, see it so.

ANTIGONE:
They see it as I do; they merely sealed their lips
in submission to you.

CREON:
      Are you not ashamed
to go against them, to differ so from the rest?

ANTIGONE:
There is nothing shameful in honouring a brother,
one's own flesh and blood.

CREON:
      And what of Eteocles, 580
slain opposing him – was not he your brother?

ANTIGONE:
Brother, yes, of the same blood; the same mother
and the same father.

CREON:
>Then how can you bestow
such impious honours upon his very enemy,
and dishonour him so?

ANTIGONE:
>Eteocles, dead and buried,
will not bear witness to that.

CREON:
>He will, I assure you,
if you honour him and the traitor as equals.

ANTIGONE:
It was no base wretch but his brother who died!

CREON:
And how? Ravaging this land, while Eteocles fell
in defence of Thebes!

ANTIGONE:
>Death is death just the same, 590
and Hades expects, demands these rites for all.

CREON:
Not for the loyal and disloyal equally.

ANTIGONE:
Who knows if this deed shall be seen as pious,
as pure by those below?

CREON:
                      Never. Unthinkable.
An enemy does not become a friend in death.

ANTIGONE:
Be they friend or enemy, revered or despised,
it is not in my nature to hate the ones I love.

CREON:
Then take yourself below and love the dead,
if love you must! For so long as I live,
no woman shall hold herself above me.   600

Enter ISMENE *from the royal house, under guard.*

CHORUS:
Look, here comes Ismene, shaking, weeping,
her comely cheeks streaming with the tears
of a loving sister, her rose-red visage
cast into shade, veiled under a cloud of grief.

CREON:
You, you accursed viper, lurking inside my house,
gorging on my life-blood! If only I had known
I was nurturing twin afflictions, two rebels
against my throne. Come now, tell me,
will you admit your part in this burial,
or refuse, deny all knowledge of the crime? 610

ISMENE:
I did it, yes – and the blame, the punishment,
I will share them both, if only she allows.

ANTIGONE:
No! Neither I nor Justice could ever permit it.
You were unwilling to help, cold to my words,
and I gave you no part in the deed – nothing.

ISMENE:
But now, seeing you here beset by peril, all I wish
is to sail through this sea of troubles at your side.

ANTIGONE:
How am I to love someone who loves in words alone?
Hades and the dead below know well whose deed it is.

ISMENE:
Sister, please – do not deprive me of all honour; 620
let me die beside you, let us hallow the dead together!

ANTIGONE:
Do not try to share my death, nor claim as your own
a deed untouched by your hands.
My death will be enough.

ISMENE:
                            And for what should I live?
How could I care for life if I am robbed of you, too?

ANTIGONE:
Ask Creon. It is he you care about most.

ISMENE:
Why torment me so, when it does you no good?

ANTIGONE:
You are right – to scorn you only brings more pain.

ISMENE:
Then tell me, please, there must be some way,
even now, that I can help you?

ANTIGONE:
                          Save yourself,   630
that is all I ask. I do not begrudge your escape.

ISMENE:
O misery – must I be denied a share in your fate?

ANTIGONE:
You chose to live; I chose to die.

ISMENE:
                                But not, at least,
without protest – I pleaded with every word I could.

ANTIGONE:
You appealed to one world, and I to another.

ISMENE:
Yet guilty are we both, two equally in the wrong.

ANTIGONE:
Take heart, Ismene! You will live – but I,
I gave myself over to death long ago,
to Hades my life in service of the dead.

CREON:
Fools, the both of them – I dare say even mad.   640
One has just revealed it; the other, in truth,
has been this way from the day she was born.

ISMENE:
It is true, my king, that the good sense endowed
in us all by nature seldom endures the worst,
and in moments of hardship, the most dire straits,
reason oft abandons the mind.

CREON:
>Yours did, clearly,
when you allied yourself in lawlessness with her.

ISMENE:
But what would life be for me, alone, without her?

CREON:
Speak of her no more, for she is already gone.

ISMENE:
What? Would you truly kill your own son's bride? 650

CREON:
Why not? There are other fields for him to plough.

ISMENE:
But none so well-matched, nor as beloved as she.

CREON:
My son, wed to some wayward harpy? Never.

ISMENE:
O dearest Hæmon, how your father wrongs you!

CREON:
Enough! Enough of you and your talk of marriage.

ISMENE:
Do you truly mean to rob your son of his love?

CREON:
It is Death who will end this marriage for me.

ISMENE:
So it is decided, then – Antigone is to die?

CREON:
Decided, yes – as we both knew it would.
No more delays. Guards, take them inside.   660
From now on they are to behave as women,
kept under watch and ward, no more running wild.
It is known that even the bravest will seek to flee,
steal away in haste when they feel Hades near,
his grasp upon them, death closing on their lives.

> *The guards lead* ISMENE *and* ANTIGONE
> *into the royal house.*

CHORUS:
Blessed are those who in all their days
taste not the bitterness of devastation.
For once the gods have shaken a house,
the ruin, unending, every kind of misery,
spreads throughout and overtakes the family, 670
cascading from one generation to the next;
like a surging tide, cresting, driven forth
by the savage breath of Thracian winds,
rolling, heaving over the deathly black,
Erebusian deep, hauling from the depths
dark clouds of sand, and the windswept headlands,
bearing the brunt of the storm's thrashing,
groan at the onslaught, a mournful roar.

Thus the sorrows of this ancient house,
the troubled line of Laius and his kin, echo 680
into the present, and the woes of the living
are heaped upon the woes of the dead.
Each generation, bound to the last, is helpless
to set the next free – the wrath of the gods
endures, and the bloodline can find no release.
And now that budding glimmer of light,
a hope, though faint, spreading from the last root
in the house of Oedipus – that fledgling flame
has been smothered under blood-stained dust,
extinguished by the gods of the underworld, 690
by mindless words, by fury of the heart.

*O mighty Zeus whose shield is thunder, what man
could defy you, who could ever restrain your power?
A power that neither Sleep, the all-ensnaring,
nor the unceasing months of the heavens
can overcome. Undiminished through time,
you reign over all from the snow-crowned peaks,
master of the gold-bright brilliance of Olympus.
Forevermore, in the future both distant and near,
as throughout the past, this law shall prevail:* 700
*in the lives of mortal men, everything – the great,
the beautiful, the vast – all must eventually fall.*

*For hope propels the loftiest of man's ambitions,
a boon to his dreams, ever-roaming far and wide;
yet for many it is the sound of the Siren's song,
a false lure, leading them into foolish desires,
enthralled by the deception as it slowly grows
and overtakes them, till at last, oblivious,
they place their feet upon the burning fire.
Wise, indeed, was the one who first spoke* 710
*that famous saying: "sooner or later,
evil will seem good, good will seem evil
to him whose mind the gods lead to ruin".
For only the briefest, most fleeting of moments
will he fare free before meeting his doom.*

Enter HAEMON *from the royal house*

Look, it is Hæmon, the last of your sons.
Does he come grieving for ill-fated Antigone,
bitter at the loss of his promised bride,
his hopes of marriage, bed and maiden, dashed?

CREON:
We shall know soon enough – no need for seers. 720

Turning to address HAEMON.

My son, tell me, do you know of the final judgement
passed upon your bride, the law that was broken?
Have you come now in a rage against your father,
or do I have your loyalty, whatever action I take?

HAEMON:
Father, I am your son – I know the wisdom
of your words. They have kept me always
upon the right path, and I heed them still.
No marriage could ever mean more to me,
be more important than you, your guidance.

CREON:
Good, Hæmon, that is how you should feel, 730
ready and willing to stand behind your father,
loyal in all matters. It is for this that men pray:

to beget many dutiful and devoted sons
who will defend their father from his enemies,
requite his foes and repay what is merited,
and honour his friends as their own.
But the man who begets only useless children,
what has he sown, I ask, save trouble for himself
and no end of mockery from his enemies?
Hæmon, my boy, you must never allow yourself 740
to be deceived by a woman, never abandon reason
for the pleasure she brings. The burning passion,
the warmth of her embrace – all of it, fleeting,
grows cold in your arms, a worthless wife
to share your bed and home. For what wound
cuts deeper than a loved one turned against you?
No, be rid of her, banish her from your thoughts
as though she were an enemy – let this girl go,
let her find a husband among the dead in Hades.
Remember that she, and she alone of all the city, 750
defied the order – openly. I shall not be made a liar
in the eyes of my people. She must pay with her life.
So let her invoke the gods, let her sing in praise
of Zeus who protects all bonds of kindred blood.
For if I should raise rebels, nurture disorder
in my own kin, how would the city view me?
Would others not do the same? The answer is clear.
For he who rules his household well, is just
in private matters, will be virtuous in the eyes
of his fellow citizens, a man to admire, a man 760

they trust will be upright in public as well.
There is no doubt in my mind that such a man
would command no less admirably than he serves,
that in a storm of spears, he would stand his ground,
dauntless in battle, a loyal brother in arms.
But whoever the city may place in power,
his rule must be obeyed, his demands followed,
in matters both great and small, just and unjust.
While whoever defies his orders, violates the law,
or presumes to dictate to his leaders, 770
no praise will he earn from me. Far from it.
For there exists no greater evil than anarchy:
she lays waste to cities, tears homes asunder,
breaks the allied ranks and throws the spearmen
into headlong rout. But most who are able
to weather the storm, they owe their lives
to discipline and deference to authority.
To this end we must always safeguard order –
never can we allow a woman to defeat us.
Better to fall from power, if ever we must, 780
at the hands of a man than be disgraced,
looked upon as weaker than a woman.

CHORUS:
Unless old age has deprived us of our wits,
you seem to speak wisely, there's sense in what you say.

HAEMON:
Father, though the gods endow man with reason,
the greatest of all the gifts we possess,
I am neither able, nor in truth do I wish,
to say how your words may be wrong.
Perhaps, however, there are others who could,
whose thoughts we might find to be of use. 790
Regardless, it is my duty to watch and listen,
to observe on your behalf what the people do,
what they say, what they find to criticise.
For fear of your gaze, the man on the street
speaks seldom such words as may displease you.
Yet murmurings I hear, whispers in the dark,
how the city weeps with grief for this girl.
"No woman", they say, "ever deserved death less,
the worst of punishments for the most noble of deeds.
She, who when her brother fell in bloody battle, 800
refused to let his body lie unburied, exposed,
to become carrion for the wild dogs and birds.
It is not death she merits, but the praise of all,
a gleaming wreath of gold!" Such is the talk
behind closed doors, an outcry silently spreading.
I assure you, father, there is no greater treasure,
nothing I value more than your prosperity –
for what honour is more precious to a child
than the wide renown of a thriving father,
or to a father the pride in his child? 810

But do not, I ask, bind yourself to one view,
or insist that it is right and all else must be wrong.
For whoever believes that he alone is wise,
that in speech and thought he has no peer,
such men, it must be said, often show themselves
to be of little substance, puffed up with bluster.
It brings a man no shame, however shrewd he may be,
to learn from others, to be willing to relent.
Think of how along the banks of winter torrents
the trees which sway, yielding to the stream, 820
preserve their branches, whilst the rigid perish,
ripped from the earth, swept, roots and all, away.
Likewise when a shipmaster hauls tight his sail,
never slackens the sheets – rough wind, a driving gale,
will roll the ship, plunge the rowing-seats under,
and leave the crew to voyage home atop the keel.
Give way, father, and suffer your anger to ease.
I am young, I know, but if I may offer one thought:
it would be better, I suppose, if man were born wise,
infallible in all things. But since our nature 830
does not tend this way, it is best to pay heed
and learn from those with worthy advice.

CHORUS:
It is right, my king, if his words seem just
that you learn from him; and you, young Hæmon,
from your father. Both sides have spoken well.

CREON:
So men of our age are to be schooled, then,
taught lessons in wisdom by boys of his age?

HAEMON:
Only if the lesson is just. And young though I am,
judge me not by my years, but my actions.

CREON:
Such as honouring rebels and subversives? 840

HAEMON:
I would never tell anyone to honour such people.

CREON:
And yet, is the girl not seized by that very sickness?

HAEMON:
The people of Thebes would say otherwise.

CREON:
And is the city to dictate how I rule?

HAEMON:
Listen to yourself. What age do you sound now?

CREON:
Am I to rule this land by my will, or the will of others?

HAEMON:
The city does not belong to one man alone.

CREON:
Has the city not always belonged to he who rules?

HAEMON:
What a fine king you would make of a desert,
of a land whose citizens are you and you alone.   850

CREON: (to the CHORUS)
This boy, it seems, is on the side of the woman.

HAEMON:
Only if you are a woman, as my concern is for you.

CREON:
And you show this how? With unjust accusations
and insults to my rule – by opposing your own father!

HAEMON:
Because I see you going wrong, erring against justice.

CREON:
Am I wrong to respect my own authority?

HAEMON:
And what of respect for the gods, of the honours
you trampled underfoot?

CREON:
                    You pathetic child,
an utter wretch – submitting to a woman!

HAEMON:
Be that as it may, never will you find me   860
yielding to disgrace. Not now, not ever.

CREON:
Yet every word you say is on her behalf!

HAEMON:
And yours, and mine, and that of the gods below!

CREON:
Know that you will never marry her,
not while she still lives.

HAEMON:
                    Then she will die,
and her death will beget the death of another.

CREON:
What? Has it come to this now? Brazen threats?

HAEMON:
How is it a threat to question such mindless thinking?

CREON:
Enough of your callow, empty-headed wisdom.
You will regret having ever dared to lecture me.   870

HAEMON:
If you were not my father, I would think you insane.

CREON:
Cease your prattle – you slave to a woman.

HAEMON:
You wish to speak and hear nothing in reply.

CREON:
Is that so? By high Olympus, know this well:
nothing will you gain, no triumph, no joy,
for this disdain, taunting me, reviling my rule.

Shouting to his attendants.

Bring her out, that accursed girl, so she may die now,
right here before his eyes, beside her betrothed!

HAEMON:
No, no, she will not die now, not at my side —
do not even think it! Never, father, 880
never will you set eyes on my face again.
So spit your venom, indulge in your madness
with whomever can still bear to be around you.

Rushing out

CHORUS:
He is gone, my king, and with haste. Such is the temper
of a young man — heavy does grief weigh upon them.
There is no telling what he may do.

CREON:
                              Let him go.
He is free to do, to imagine some desperate act,
something far beyond the means of man.
Nothing will change the fate of those girls.

CHORUS:
Both? Do you truly intend to put both to death? 890

CREON:
No, you're quite right, not the one who is blameless,
who had no hand in the deed.

CHORUS:
                              And what of the other?
Have you decided how Antigone shall meet her end?

CREON:
I shall lead her out to some desolate spot,
along paths never trod by men, and seal her away,
entomb her alive in a deep vault of rock,
leaving her such rations as piety demands
so that the city may be spared defilement.
There she may pray to the one god she worships,
to Hades – and perhaps he will spare her this doom.   900
Or else she will learn at last, in her final hours,
how foolish, how futile it is to worship Death.

             CREON *withdraws into the royal house.*

CHORUS:
Eros, unconquered in battle;
Eros, descending upon riches;
Eros, guarding through the night
the soft cheek of a sleeping girl;
Eros, ranging the farthest seas,
haunting the highest pastures
and the deepest of wilds.
None – not even the deathless gods, 910
nor man who lives for but a day,
can flee from your advance.
All are driven mad by your grasp.

Eros, you seize the minds of good men,
warp the just and drag them into outrage,
to their ruin. You, who ignited this feud,
this kindred strife between father and son.
Yet victory belongs to desire alone,
the amorous gaze of a blushing young bride
enthroned in power beside the mighty laws! 920
And so fair Aphrodite, irresistible to all,
plays her games, mocking the hearts of men.

ANTIGONE *is led from the royal house under guard.*

But now even I, as I behold this sight,
am moved beyond the bounds of law and loyalty,
powerless to hold back these streams of tears
when I see her, Antigone, making her way
to the chamber where all must someday sleep.

ANTIGONE:
Fellow citizens, men of my fatherland,
see me as I depart on my final journey,
upon the last road, gazing at the last sunlight 930
I shall ever behold. Hades, lord of the dead,
who lays us all to rest, leads me living
to the banks of Acheron, denied the rites,
the honours bestowed on the wedding day,
no bridal hymn sung to crown my marriage
as I go to wed the lord of the sorrowing waters.

CHORUS:
Yet you leave for the depths where dwell the dead
with undying glory and the people's praise,
neither laid low by some wasting malady,
nor forced to pay the wages of the sword, 940
but of your own will – alone among mortals,
you descend to Hades alive and triumphant.

ANTIGONE:
And yet my thoughts stray to that lady of Phrygia,
of piteous Niobe, daughter of Tantalus,
how she perished upon the peaks of Sipylus,
bound by rock, enclosed, the growing stone
spreading across her flesh like clinging ivy
till unmoving she became, still forevermore;
how the rains, men say, never cease to fall,
the thawing snows never leave her frozen form,   950
and so beneath her brows the endless tears
pour upon the mountainside – a rock that ever weeps.
Thus the gods lead me, like Niobe, to my rest.

CHORUS:
Yet she was of divine blood, begotten of a god,
while we are mere mortals and of mortal birth.
Though it is, undeniably, a fine thing
for a dying girl to hear, to have it said
that she shares the destiny of a goddess,
both in life, and thereafter, in death.

ANTIGONE:
O, you mock me! In the name of our fathers' gods,   960
must you taunt me now, while still I live,
can you not hold your tongues till I am gone?
O my city, what a fine crowd of moneyed elders!
May the springs and fountains of flowing Dirce,
sacred grove of Thebes whose chariots are famed,

may you, at least, be my witnesses this day,
how unwept by friends, at the whim of godless laws,
I go to my stone-heaped prison, that unheard-of tomb.
O cruel misery – a stranger to all, no home
amidst mortals here or the shades below, 970
no home amongst the living or the dead.

CHORUS:
You pushed to the farthest limits of daring,
a reckless march, and stumbled, my child,
fell heavily before the high throne of Justice.
Perhaps you pay still for the woes of your father.

ANTIGONE:
Now you strike at my most bitter anguish,
at that which truly pains me – my father's grief,
his grim fate ever-renewed, and the dreadful ruin
brought down on us all, on the famed house of Laius.
O the horrors of that unholy marriage-bed, 980
my ill-fated mother, unwitting wife to her own son,
to my father, sleeping at his side – a union cursed
and I its wretched child. Such were my parents,
and to them I go now, condemned and unwed,
to share once more their home. O dear brother,
your ill-made marriage begot the doom of mine,
your death drags me living into the dismal gloom.

CHORUS:
Your piety is plain and worthy of honour,
but an offence against power will never be brooked,
no challenge goes unanswered by those who rule. 990
Your own wilfulness, your temper has destroyed you.

Enter CREON.

ANTIGONE:
Unmourned, unloved, without song or dirge,
they lead me away in woe along that final path.
What deep agony! No longer shall I look upon
the heavens' bright eye, forbidden to ever behold
the divine light of day. Yet none weep for my fate,
no dear friend, no loved one bewails my death.

CREON:
Do you not see that if a man were free to howl,
to wail his own funeral song before he died,
he would never stop? Take her away – at once! 1000
Wall her in, as ordered, enclose her in that vault
and leave her there, alone – let her decide
if it is death she desires, or a life entombed.
Either way, our hands are clean. Alive or dead,
she will be stripped of any home in this world.

ANTIGONE:
O tomb, cold bridal-bed, my everlasting prison
deep within the empty stone – to you I go now
to embrace my own, the many kin who came to ruin,
whom pale Persephone received amongst the dead.
I, the last of them, my descent the worst by far,   1010
go down before my life has reached its end.
Yet I leave in hope, cherishing the thought
that I may be greeted as one who is loved,
welcomed warmly by those most dear to me –
my father and mother, my brother, Eteocles.
When you perished I tended to your bodies,
washed and adorned them with my own hands,
poured sweet libations upon your graves.
But now, Polynikes, since I dared to perform
these same rites for you, this is my reward.   1020
This, when I honoured you well, as was right,
as the pious, the wise, the honest all know.

If, in truth, I had been the mother of children,
or if a husband in death had been left unburied,
never would I have defied the will of our people,
never taken this hardship upon myself.
By reason of what law, you ask, do I say this?
Were my husband to die, I might find another,
and if a child were lost, we could bear yet more.
But with mother and father both lost to Hades,   1030
no brother could ever be brought forth again.

Such was the law by which I held you first in honour,
for which, dear brother, Creon has condemned me,
judged me guilty of wrongdoing – of an outrage
most grave! And now, at the mercy of his grip,
he leads me away, denies me my part in the future,
all the joys of wedlock, the raising of children.
Thus deserted by loved ones, cursed by cruel fate,
I descend alive into the deep hollows of the dead.

O tell me, what sacred law have I transgressed? 1040
Why in my despair should I still look to the gods?
Whom do I call upon, what ally do I have?
My piety brings only the charge of impiety,
my reverence is repaid with a criminal's fate!
If this is truly pleasing to the gods, so be it.
Once I have suffered, I will know that I was wrong,
and with that I shall gladly accept my doom.
But if they are wrong, if my judges have erred,
may they suffer no less, may their punishment
befit the injustice they impose upon me! 1050

CHORUS:
Still the same tempest, the same fierce passion
raging in her soul.

CREON: *(to the guards)*
                    Be gone with you, quickly!
Tarry any longer and you shall soon regret it.

ANTIGONE:
O shrouding death – it looms in your words...

CREON:
Indeed so, and I offer you no consolation,
no hope to cling to that your doom is not sealed.

ANTIGONE:
O land of fair Thebes, city of my fathers,
you ancestral gods, flesh and blood of old,
they lead me away now, the time has come!
Look upon me, you noble men of Thebes,   1060
upon the last member of the house of Laius,
our great line of kings – see what I suffer,
and from what breed of men, all for piety,
for devotion, my reverence for the gods!

          ANTIGONE leaves under guard.

CHORUS:
Danaë, too, in all her loveliness,
was hidden away, made to surrender
the light of heaven for that brass-bound vault,
buried in her brazen tomb, her bridal chamber,
and left there, confined, wedded to her prison.

Though she, dear child, was of exalted descent, 1070
and to her Zeus granted the gift of his seed,
a gleaming cloudburst, bright stream of gold,
bestowing upon her that treasured child.

Fathomless is the power of fate,
a dark and dreadful power –
neither wealth nor strength of arms,
towering walls nor black-hulled ships
can defy that almighty force.

So it was for the fierce-tempered son of Dryas,
Lycurgus, king of Edonia, ever swift to rage, 1080
brought under the yoke for his wrathful taunts,
shut away, enclosed by twice-born Dionysus
in a prison of rock. There his terrible fury,
his burgeoning madness burst, bloomed and withered,
fading slowly, ebbing away until at last
he came to understand the power of the god
he had provoked, disdained in his frenzy.
For he had sought to extinguish the Bacchic fire,
to quell the raving mænads, their wild devotion,
angering the Muses who delight in the flute. 1090

And beside the twin seas where the Dark Rocks clash,
where narrow straits sunder the shores of Thrace,
in the halls of wind-bitten Salmydessus,
Ares beheld that vicious attack, the blinding
of the sons of Phineus, schemed and wrought
by the king's new wife, that accursed harpy
weaving her lies – with the crimson shuttle,
a dagger gripped in her bloodstained hands,
she pierced their eyes, plunged both hollows
into everlasting night, the two princes, maimed,
crying out, craving vengeance for their wounds.

Wasting away in misery, chained and fettered,
they bewailed their doom, born of a mother
banished from her marriage and cast into irons,
imprisoned, unwed, beneath a barrow of stone.
But she, fair Cleopatra, traced her descent
from a proud and ancient Athenian line,
born from the blood of great Erechtheus
and nurtured amongst the caves of distant lands,
riding upon the gales of her fierce father,
winged Boreas, god of the northern winds,
swift as a stallion over the climbing hills she flew,
a daughter of the gods. Yet even she, dear child,
was bridled, pressed hard by the eternal Fates.

Enter the blind seer, TIRESIAS, *led by a boy.*

TIRESIAS:
Lords of Thebes, together we have come to you,
a shared path, two seeing with the eyes of one.
For so the blind go, with another to guide the way.

CREON:
What is it, wise Tiresias? What news?

TIRESIAS:
I shall tell you – and you shall heed the seer.

CREON:
Of course. Never have I strayed from your counsel.

TIRESIAS:
And that is why you steered this city aright,
kept her on a straight course.

CREON:
                      I do not deny it,
experience has shown me your wisdom.

TIRESIAS:
Then know this: you stand once more, poised
upon the razor's edge of grim fate.

CREON:
What is it? I shudder to hear you speak this way.

TIRESIAS:
You will learn, my boy, when you hear the omens
revealed by my craft. For as I sat upon that ancient
seat of augury, a haven for those who divine,
where the birds of prey all gather before me, 1130
I heard it, suddenly, a strange and awful cry,
a voice amidst the frenzied beating of wings,
unintelligible, barbaric to my ears!
The birds, their talons athirst for blood,
were tearing at each other, intent, I knew,
upon dealing death, the grim rush of feathers
unmistakable, a clear and terrible sign.
Fearful, I sought at once to test a burnt-offering,
the flames all duly kindled upon the altar stone,
but from my offerings Hephæstus took nothing, 1140
the sacred fire failed to blaze. Over the embers
a thick slime oozed, slid from the thighbones,
smoking and sputtering; the bladder burst apart,
scattering gall into the air, and the fat, still raw,
that had enveloped the bones merely fell away,
leaving them bare, white in the foreboding flame.
Such were my efforts to divine an answer,
the failure of the rites, as I learned from this boy.
For he is my guide, as I am a guide to others.

And it is your will, Creon, your judgement
that has brought this sickness upon the city.
The altars and hearths, one and all, are sullied,
defiled by the birds and dogs with carrion,
foul flesh torn from the fallen son of Oedipus!
And so the gods accept our prayers no longer,
they are cold to our flame, our burnt-offerings;
while the shrieking birds, disturbed in call and flight,
give no clear omens, glutted as they are
on the blood-soaked fat of a slain man.
Consider these things, my son, take them to heart.
All men err, for such is the nature of man.
But once the mistake is made, he may choose
to put his folly and misfortune behind him,
to admit his error and right the wrong done,
however far he has fallen – if only he relents,
if he does not hold to his headstrong ways.
For stubbornness invites the charge of folly,
blind pride makes a wretch of us all.
                                        Give way,
yield to the dead! Do not stab at a man
veiled in darkness. What glory can be won,
what valour is there in slaying the dead again?
I mean you well, and well have I counselled you.
It is worthwhile to learn from a good adviser
when his words are spoken for your good.

CREON:
Old man, all of you, you shoot your arrows at me
like bowmen at a target – even the prophetic arts are
loosed against me. You and your scheming ilk,
the whole coin-clutching tribe of fortune-tellers,
for years you have made a gainful trade of me,
shipped me around like cheap merchandise.					1180
So traffic your wares, profit as you wish, barter
for the pale gold of Sardis, the gold of India –
never will you bury that man in a grave,
not even if the eagles of Zeus himself
should tear at the corpse, snatch up the rotting flesh
and wing their spoils away, up to Olympus,
gorging themselves beside his high throne.
                                                    No,
not even then, not for fear of such defilement
would I allow that traitor to be buried.
For I know well that no man, no mortal					1190
has the power to defile the gods.
All men do indeed err, old Tiresias,
but the wisest fall most shamefully
when they dignify ignoble thinking
with fine words – and all for profit's sake.

TIRESIAS:

                                           Alas,
is there a man who knows, who understands—

CREON:
Understands what? What profound truth
are you proclaiming now?

TIRESIAS:

                       —by how much prudence,
sound judgement is the greatest of our gifts?

CREON:
By as much, I suppose, as a witless mind,
as imprudence is the worst of our afflictions.

TIRESIAS:
And yet you are infected with that very sickness.

CREON:
I have no desire to trade insults with a seer.

TIRESIAS:
Yet you already have, for you were more than happy
to brand my prophecies a lie.

CREON:
>Why wouldn't I?
All seers, the whole breed, are devoted to money.

TIRESIAS:
And all tyrants are ruled by their lust for gain.

CREON:
Are you aware that you're speaking to your ruler?

TIRESIAS:
Quite aware. For it was through me, my help
that you saved this city.

CREON:
>You have your skills, seer, 1210
but your love of injustice has led you astray.

TIRESIAS:
You will push me to say what is best left unsaid,
what I had hoped to keep in my heart.

CREON:
Out with it! But do not speak for profit.

TIRESIAS:
No, there shall be no profit, not in these words.

CREON:
Just know that you cannot barter for my resolve.

TIRESIAS:
Then know this, Creon, pay close heed:
the swift chariot of the racing sun
shall not finish many circuits more
ere you surrender one born from your loins, 1220
blood for blood, a corpse in return for corpses.
For you have thrust down, cast into shade
one who belongs amidst the light of day,
wrongly entombed a living soul in the grave;
while another you hold here, exposed to the sky,
one whose rightful home is with the gods below,
a body unburied, unmourned, unhallowed.
You have no part in this, no business with the dead,
nor do the gods above – but you have forced it,
forced this outrage upon the heavens. 1230
And so the grim Furies, fell daughters of Night,
now lie in wait for you, the avenging Erinyes
sent forth by Hades and the high gods
to visit upon you the very woes you wrought.
Do these strike you still as the words of one
who speaks for silver? Think well on this,
for the hour draws near, a tell not long in time,
when the sound of weeping shall fill your halls,
pained cries of lament, mourning men and women.

A great uproar shall spread amongst the cities,   1240
fierce hatred swelling, rising up against you,
the torn and mangled bodies of their sons
graced by the dogs and beasts with burial,
or seized upon by the scavenging birds
that wing the ungodly stench of carrion
back to each city, to their sacred hearths and homes.
There you have it, the keen arrows for your heart,
loosed in anger, and like an archer finding his foe,
for all your disdain, your maddening insults,
I let them fly straight and true for their target –   1250
never shall you escape their burning sting.

Gesturing to the boy, his guide.

Come, child, lead me home, let him vent his rage
against younger men, and perhaps he may learn
to quieten his tongue, to think with more sense
than the folly which beclouds his mind now.

Exit TIRESIAS.

CHORUS:
He is gone, my lord – such awful prophecies.
And well I know that in all my days,
crowned as I am with white hair once black, never
has he uttered a falsehood to our city.

CREON:
I know it myself – it troubles me deeply. 1260
It is a terrible thing to yield, give way,
but to resist now and lay myself open
to the blows of ruin – what terror that stirs.

CHORUS:
Now more than ever, you must seek good counsel.

CREON:
What should I do? Speak and I shall obey.

CHORUS:
Go, free the girl at once from her chamber-grave,
raise a burial mound over the body you exposed.

CREON:
This is your counsel? You believe I should give in?

CHORUS:
Yes, my king, and with haste, for those sent by the gods,
the swift-winged Harms, cut short the wrongs of man, 1270
untarrying in their flight.

CREON:
                    How hard it is
to abandon the heart's resolve – but I shall do it.
No sense in waging a vain war with necessity.

CHORUS:
Then do it now, go – do not leave this to others.

CREON:
I depart this moment – come, all of you, every man,
take up axes, make at once for that place,
you see it there, on the high ground, hurry!
For the better my judgement has turned –
I walled her in, and I shall set her free myself.
I admit, though not without fear, that it is best   1280
to observe the old laws passed down to us
always and ever, to the very day we die.

> CREON *and his men rush out.*

CHORUS:
*O god of many names! Glory of fair Semele,
kin of Cadmus, son of loud-thundering Zeus!
You who guard that far-famed land,*
> *Italia of the evening gold;*
*Lord of the Mysteries, reigning in Eleusis,
sheltered vales of Demeter where all find welcome!
O Bacchus of the flowing wine, denizen of Thebes,
motherland of the dancing, frenzied Bacchæ,
dwelling beside the waters of swift Ismenus,*   1290
upon the soil where the dragon's teeth were sown!

*We see the smoky flames, your torches blazing
above the twin peaks, that double-crested cliff
where the Corycian nymphs step with Bacchic zeal,
We see you at the silver spring of Castalia,
and on the ivy-rich slopes of Nysa's hills,
the spring-green coast awash with grapes and vines,
as you lead your followers down, down upon Thebes
to watch over and ward the streets of our city,
the ecstatic cries sounding your way!* 1300

*Thebes of all cities you hold first in honour
with your mother, bride of the bright thunderbolt.
And now the citizens, your people are gripped
by a dreadful plague, you must come, Dionysus,
come with your cleansing, healing stride
over the steep slopes of Parnassus,
or across the groaning blue narrows!*

*O leader of the chorus, lord of the dancing stars,
the sky alight with their revelling breath of fire!
Conductor of the night's merry voices!* 1310
*Child of the lightning, son of high Zeus,
come forth, come to us, Saviour, Liberator,
come with your whirling, raving nymphs,
singing and dancing till the night burns away,
a frenzied dance in devotion to you,
Iacchus, giver of plenty, giver of all!*

Enter a MESSENGER.

MESSENGER:
Neighbours of the house of Cadmus and Amphion,
there is nothing, no state in this mortal life
that I would ever praise or blame as settled.
Fortune raises and Fortune sinks the lucky 1320
and unlucky each day – and no one, no prophet,
can foretell all that is destined for man.
Take Creon, our king: there, as I once saw it,
was a man to be envied – he guarded our city,
saved the land of Cadmus from its enemies,
claimed sole command, mastery of Thebes,
and guided her aright; he flourished at the head
of a noble family, glorying in his sons –
and now it has all been lost.
                          What remains?
For it seems that when a man has lost his joys, 1330
he lives not, but lasts, a corpse that still draws breath.
Pile up riches in your home, heap them high,
live, if you so wish, with a tyrant's pomp,
but if there is no delight, no happiness to be had,
I would give not the shadow of smoke for it all,
not compared with joy – true, abiding joy.

CHORUS:
What new grief do you bring the royal house?

MESSENGER:
Dead – they are dead. And the living are guilty
of their deaths.

CHORUS:
                Who has been slain?
Who is the murderer? Tell us, speak plainly.   1340

MESSENGER:
Hæmon is dead, his blood shed by the very hand–

CHORUS:
His father's, or his own?

MESSENGER:
                     His own, in a fury,
enraged with his father for the murder–

CHORUS:
O great seer, it has come to pass – how true,
how terrible your word!

MESSENGER:
                  That is what happened;
what must be done now is for you to consider.

                As he turns to leave, EURYDICE *appears*
                        from inside the royal house.

CHORUS:
Look, I see poor Eurydice, Creon's wife,
so close by. Either she comes here by chance,
or she has heard us, heard the news of her son.

EURYDICE:
All of you, men of Thebes – as I made to leave, 1350
departing for the shrine of Pallas Athena
to offer her my prayers, I caught your words.
I had but loosened the bolts, reaching forward
to push the door open, when a voice of grief,
of sorrow upon this house, struck my ears –
at once, overcome by terror, my senses fled;
I fell back into the arms of my maidservants,
and all went black. But whatever was said,
speak it once more and I shall listen,
for sorrow and I are well acquainted. 1360

MESSENGER:
My dear lady, I shall speak of what I witnessed;
not a word of the truth shall be left untold.
For what good would it do to soothe you with words
that would soon be found false, make of me a liar?
No, the truth is always best.
                            Here is what happened:
I followed your husband, accompanied him
to the plain's peak where the body of Polynikes
still lay unpitied, torn, ripped apart by dogs.

After we had prayed, entreating Pluto
and Hecate, lady of the crossroads,   1370
to show us mercy and hold back their anger,
we washed the body, cleansed it with water,
and burned what was left of him together
upon a pyre of fresh-plucked olive boughs,
raising a high mound of his native earth.
Then we turned towards her prison of stone,
the hollow chamber of Hades' young bride.
From afar, one of the men heard a voice,
a grim wailing from that unhallowed tomb,
and came in haste to inform lord Creon.   1380
We continued on, and as the king drew near,
the strange, anguished cry grew louder, sharper,
enveloping him, till suddenly he halted, let forth
a despairing cry, his words a bitter, bleak lament:
"O harsh fate, am I to be the prophet now?
Do I tread upon the path most wretched of all
I have ever walked? My son – my dear son,
it is him, his voice that greets me.

                                      Men, hurry!
Go on ahead, quickly – when you reach the tomb,
enter where the stones have been dragged aside,   1390
make your way to the vault's very mouth
and see if it is Hæmon's voice I hear,
or if the gods have deceived me".
At the desperate commands of our lord,
we set off at once, searched through the dark,

and there, in the furthest depths of the tomb,
amidst stone draped in shade, we found her, the girl,
hanged by her neck in a fine linen noose,
bound in death, strangled by her woven veil;
while the boy, embracing her, his trembling arms 1400
wrapped about her waist, clung to her still body,
grieving the loss of his bride to the dead below,
bewailing his father's deeds, his doomed marriage.
When Creon saw him, he let out a dreadful cry
then rushed forward, howling, calling to him:
"O reckless child, what have you done?
What folly seized you? By what cruel thread of fate
were you drawn into madness?
                    O gods...
Come out, my son, come now, I beg of you!"
But Hæmon merely glared at him with a wild look, 1410
a fierce loathing in his eyes; without a word in reply,
he drew his blade, and as his father turned to flee,
rushing out, he lunged for him, yet the blow missed.
Beside himself, despairing at his rage, his doom,
he bent forward suddenly upon his sword
and drove the keen edge deep into his body,
burying the blade half-way to its grip.
As his life ebbed away, he pulled the girl close,
enfolding her in his waning embrace;
his breathing grew heavy, and gasping 1420
he sent forth a sharp stream of blood,
dark drops of crimson upon her ivory cheek.

And there he lay, corpse holding corpse,
united with his bride in marriage at last –
not here, poor boy, but in the house of Hades.
Creon has shown us the price of imprudence,
why thoughtless judgement is the worst of man's ills.

> EURYDICE *turns and walks back
> inside the royal house.*

CHORUS:
What do you think of that? The lady has gone,
back inside without a word, good or bad.

MESSENGER:
I, too, am surprised. My only thought, my hope, 1430
is that faced with the grave news of her son,
she thinks it unbecoming to lament in public,
to give vent to her grief before us all.
Inside, however, in the shelter of her home,
she may mourn the sorrow of their house,
weep freely in the company of her handmaids.
For she is far too practised in discretion,
too prudent to err.

CHORUS:
                Perhaps you are right.
Yet to my mind, a heavy, unbroken silence
spells trouble no less than unbridled weeping. 1440

MESSENGER:
We must know if she was holding back, hiding
some terrible passion in her grief-stricken heart.
I shall go inside at once, for you speak the truth;
even silence itself can be a sign of trouble.

The MESSENGER *enters the royal house.*

CREON *arrives with his men, carrying the
shrouded body of* HAEMON *on a bier.*

CHORUS:
Look, now the king himself approaches,
bearing in his hands a token, clear proof –
if it is right to say it – of the madness,
the fatal wrongs that were his and his alone.

CREON:
Curse the misdeeds of unthinking minds,
senseless and stubborn, yielding only death!   1450
O men of Thebes, look upon us, behold,
two kinsmen, flesh and blood, killer and killed!
What misery born of my laws, my words...
O my child, my dear son, gone, dead so young!
You depart this world, your life cut short,
not by your own foolishness, but by mine.

CHORUS:
Alas, you see too late what justice is.

CREON:
O, I have learned, and what a bitter lesson!
Some god, it seemed, had struck me blind,
a mighty blow that robbed me of my senses,   1460
driving me down wild and ruinous paths,
overturning, trampling my joy under foot!
How cruel and toilsome is the lot of mortals!

The MESSENGER *returns.*

MESSENGER:
My lord, you have come laden with woe enough,
but the grief that you bear beside you–

Glancing towards the body of HAEMON.

–there is more, I'm afraid, inside the house.
You shall see it for yourself, and all too soon.

CREON:
What now? What new misery is there left?

MESSENGER:
Your wife, lady Eurydice, is dead.
The mother of your son, of this corpse –
the poor woman, her wounds still fresh.

CREON:
                        No...

O harbour of Hades, hardest to purge,
to cleanse – why, why do you destroy me so?
Herald of grief, what new pain is this you utter?
You drive the blade into a man already slain!
What are you saying, boy? What news is this?
O accursed torment! My wife is dead?
Fresh slaughter heaped upon slaughter,
ruin upon ruin without end?

The doors of the royal house open as the body of EURYDICE *is carried out.*

CHORUS:
                    Look, my king,
the hard truth, no longer hidden, but in sight.

CREON:
O gods, I see it, a second spear to my heart.
What more must I endure, what fate still awaits me?

I just held my son in these wretched arms,
and now before me I see another corpse –
O anguished mother! O heartsick child!

MESSENGER:
At the altar, my lord, she stabbed herself,
struck deep with a sharp-whetted blade,
weeping till darkness fell upon her eyes.
First she had mourned the noble fate of Megareus,
killed in defence of Thebes, then poor Hæmon, 1490
and with her dying breath she called down
torments upon you, the slayer of her sons—

CREON:
O please, no more – such chilling words.
Why not strike me down, plunge a sharp sword
straight through my flesh and grant me release?
Dear gods, I can fall no further, I have sunk
to the very depths of woe, entwined with misery.

MESSENGER:
–for she, lying dead now before us, held you to blame,
condemned you for their deaths, the doom of her sons.

CREON:
How did she depart? What was the fatal moment? 1500

MESSENGER:
After learning of her son's grim fate,
hearing the lamentations in her home,
she struck to the heart with her own hand.

CREON:
Alas, this guilt is mine, it belongs to me alone,
no other man can bear this blame – it was I,
yes, I who killed you, wretched that I am,
I admit it, all of it, the awful truth!
Take me away, quickly, lead me out of sight – I
who live no more, who am less than nothing.

CHORUS:
Good advice, if there can be good amidst such ill. 1510
Best to move quickly when faced with the worst.

CREON: *(placing his hands together in prayer)*
Come, let it come, may the best of fates
come forth for me, may it bring my final day,
that finest fate of all! Come, let it come,
so I never have to see another day!

CHORUS:
Such matters belong to the future –
we must take care of what lies before us;
all else rests in the hands of those it should.

CREON:
I have prayed for all that I desire.

CHORUS:
Then pray no more – for man there is no escape, 1520
no release from the hard threads of fate long spun.

CREON:
Lead me away, I beg of you, take this fool,
this rash, impious fool far away from here!

> *Looking back and forth in desperation
> at the bodies of* HAEMON *and* EURYDICE.

Unwilling, unthinking, I murdered you, my son,
and you, too, my dear wife...
                     O the agony –
where do I look, to whom can I turn for solace?
All that I touch comes to grief, and once more
a crushing doom has struck down upon me.

> CREON *is lead by his men into the royal house.*

CHORUS:
Wisdom is the greatest pillar of happiness,
and ever must the gods be held in reverence. 1530
The mighty words of the proud are punished,
repaid in full with mighty blows of fate,
till at long last they teach men wisdom.

FAMILY
&
FATHERLAND

FAMILY & FATHERLAND
ON THE HISTORY AND THEMES OF SOPHOCLES' ANTIGONE

Antigone, one of Sophocles' earliest extant works, is believed to have been composed during or shortly before the year 441 B.C., placing it at the very heart of the age of Periclean Athens. The playwright was a prominent figure in the city-state at this time: in 443 B.C. he was appointed to the board of public treasurers, the *Hellenotamiæ*, and two years later, he served alongside Pericles as a general in the Samos campaign. Yet Sophocles' greatest contribution to this golden period in Athenian history was of course his tragedies. Appropriately, and doubtless reflecting the spirit of the hour, the marble columns of the Parthenon were gradually rising upon the Acropolis at this time – a fine backdrop for the first performance of *Antigone*.

The enduring appeal of Sophocles' works bespeak both his understanding of the human condition, informed, no doubt, by his many exceptional contemporaries, and his ability to communicate and elevate the tribulations and triumphs of mortal life through art. This is true of none more so than

Antigone. That the play continues to captivate audiences and inspire discussion to this day, millennia after the crowning peaks of classical Greek civilisation ebbed and waned to its close, is proof enough, perhaps, that as Hegel was compelled to proclaim, *Antigone* is "one of the most sublime, and in every respect most consummate works of art human effort has ever produced".[1]

Before any exploration of the play and its themes may be undertaken, however, it is imperative that we first understand the time and place in which its author was situated, the currents of thought which inspired the play's creation. For Sophocles, this was fifth century Athens, a flourishing city-state, growing empire, and, not insignificantly, a democracy. One should be careful, of course, not to project modern Western conceptions of democracy onto its Ancient Greek progenitor, for while the city fostered a remarkable degree of intellectual and artistic freedom compared to most of its contemporaries, such notions as universal suffrage and unqualified egalitarianism were distinctly absent. Only free men of Athenian birth who had completed their military service were permitted to participate in politics – women, slaves, and foreign settlers were excluded entirely. Moreover, the charge of impiety (ἀσέβεια) was not uncommon during this period: prominent tragedians Aeschylus

---

1. Hegel, *Philosophy of Fine Art*

and Euripides both gained acquittals, while Socrates was famously sentenced to death. Freedom of inquiry or expression had their limits, and as the notoriously questioning philosopher discovered, being seen to spread moral corruption or irreverence towards the gods of the city was not to be tolerated, even in Athens.

Alongside these very particular notions of liberty and popular political participation, the democracy in which Sophocles lived was based around several core principles, including family, ancestry, nativism, and loyalty to the city-state. It was also an unapologetically patriarchal society which valued military courage as one of the highest virtues – both features typical of a Traditional culture. In his famous Funeral Oration, delivered less than ten years after the composition of *Antigone*, Pericles spoke the following before a public gathering in honour of the Athenian dead:

> "I shall begin with our ancestors, for it is right and appropriate on such an occasion that this tribute should be paid to their memory. The same race has always occupied this land, handing it down from generation to generation until the present day, and it is to these brave men that we owe our inheritance of a land that is free...you must yourselves realise the power of Athens, and look upon her day after day, till love of her fills your hearts"[1]

---

1. Thucydides, *The Peloponnesian War*, 2.36, 2.43

To this we may add a few lines from Aeschylus' *Persians*, a play financed in part by Pericles which recounts Athens' great victory over the invading Persian fleet at Salamis:

> "on, you sons of Hellas! Free your fatherland,
> free your children, your wives, the temples of
> your paternal gods, and the tombs of your
> ancestors! You are fighting now for all you have!"[1]

We see, then, that the free and just society which Athens championed was underpinned by a fervent patriotism rooted in kinship and lineage, to which the worship of the gods was intrinsically linked. The importance placed upon family and fatherland, not only during times of war, but in the general ordering of society was long established: it far predated the development of the Greek city-state, and endured seemingly undiminished into the Classical era. The question that must be asked, however, and which Sophocles has presented as central to the conflict of *Antigone*, is what happens when family and fatherland are disunited; when loyalty to one's kin and state are at variance. Or, as we shall discover, when the civic institution of the state places itself at odds with the religious tradition of its people.

For the ancients, the "inspiring breath and organiser of society"[2] at every level was religion.

---

1. Aeschylus, *Persians*, 402   2. Fustel de Coulanges, *The Ancient City*

Traditional man oriented himself towards the sacred, wherefore his daily life and the world about him were imbued with a religious significance. At the centre of his home, itself often inherited from his forefathers and preserved for his descendants, was a fixed hearth, around which so much of ancient domestic life revolved. The hearth, preserve of the goddess Hestia who watched over the family, was the sacred heart of the Greek household: every morning and evening the family would gather to address their prayers before it; and for each meal, they would assemble beside it, partaking of their food after prayer and libation, with an offering made first to the flame. The hearth-fire, ever-burning, was symbolic of an eternal horizon, rooted deep in the past and one's belonging within the great chain of existence. The family linked its members to all that had come before, and all that was to follow, an "immortal community"[1] bound by blood and the timeless rites shared by all.

The veneration of ancestors was central to Greek paganism, as it was to all Indo-European religions; at their household altar, they made offerings not merely to the pantheon of gods with whom we are well-acquainted, but to their forefathers, the spirits whom they honoured, whom they believed could still influence the world of the living, and with whom they would one day be reunited in the underworld.

---

1. Ahrensdorf, *Greek Tragedy and Political Philosophy*

The dead, it was believed, could aid the living who honoured them, or plague the neglectful as malevolent spirits. In *The Libation Bearers*, for instance, Electra addresses a prayer to her father in which she entreats him to help both her and her brother, and to ensure that vengeance is brought upon his killers:

> "I pour these libations to the dead, I invoke my father...O bring Orestes home and with good fortune. Hear me, grant that I may be more self-possessed than my mother, make this hand more pure, more reverent in deed. These prayers I utter for us. For our enemies, raise up your avenger into the light so that the killers may be killed in return, with justice!"[1]

The worship of the gods was enshrined alongside a deep reverence for the dead – specifically one's ancestors – and the mutual obligations of kinship were retained even in death. The family altar was carefully kept, and it was considered a sacred duty for the head of the household to maintain the hearth-fire, and thus the blessings of Hestia, both night and day:

> "woe to the house where it was extinguished. Every evening they covered the coals with ashes to prevent them from being entirely consumed; in the morning, the first care was to revive this fire with a

---

1. Aeschylus, *The Libation Bearers*, 128-50

few twigs. The fire ceased to glow upon the altar only when the entire family had perished – an extinguished hearth, an extinguished family were synonymous expressions among the ancients"[1]

Indeed, after some twenty years estranged from his home, Odysseus returned to Ithaca to be reunited with his wife Penelope, who had remained faithful to him and preserved the "hearth's unwearied fire",[2] thereby safeguarding the family.

For the ancient Greeks, then, religion and family were deeply intertwined – indivisible, even – and many of the principles which guided their lives were replicated in public life. As the house rose around the domestic hearth, so too the city rose around the civic hearth: the rites, health, and ordering of both presided over by Hestia, the goddess and her flame enthroned amongst the highest gods in the pantheon of the polis. As Plato, another Athenian, outlined for the founding of his ideal city,[3] the first act, after dividing the land into twelve portions, was to establish a fortified sanctuary for Zeus, Athena, and Hestia known as the ἀκρόπολις (Acropolis; literally the "upper city" or "citadel").

In accordance with the particularism of domestic worship, the gods of each city-state were regarded as belonging especially to that polis, to its soil and

---

1. Coulanges, *The Ancient City* 2. *The Odyssey*, XX, 123
3. Plato, *Laws*, 5.745b

people. Therefore, while Zeus, for instance, was recognisably the same deity across the Hellenic world, the relationship between a god and a given city would often be seen as distinct:

> "each of these gods, like the Juno of Virgil, had the grandeur of his city at heart. These gods had the same interests as the citizens themselves, and in times of war marched to battle in the midst of them" [1]

Just as the home was inherited from the family's forefathers whom they reverenced and received protection from, so the founder of a city, be they historical or mythological, was believed to be of divine parentage, and thus the noble families claimed descent from the god or gods who guarded the city:

> "O land of fair Thebes, city of my fathers,
> you ancestral gods, flesh and blood of old"[2]

To wage war against a city was to wage war against its gods. Consequently, when the Greeks besieged a city, they would often address an invocation to its gods and ancestral heroes in order to win their favour and thereby ensure victory.[3] It follows that to betray one's city was to betray one's gods, an act unthinkable given

---

1. Coulanges, *The Ancient City*   2. 1057-8
3. Thucydides, *The Peloponnesian War*, 2.74

the relationship between kinship, citizenship, and religion for the ancients.

The fatherland of every Greek stood upon ground sanctified by his religion, upon the very soil where the remains of his ancestors were buried. The little fatherland was his family home with its tomb and hearth; the great fatherland was his city, with its town hall and communal hearth, its heroes, its sacred enclosure, and its boundaries marked out by religious rite.[1] All that man held dear was associated with his country: his kin, his gods, his property, his safety, his laws, his inheritance, his legacy. As Creon proclaims, "the city is our home, our deliverance, our prosperity"[2] and as Plato echoed, "our country begets us, nourishes us, elevates us".[3] To lose his fatherland was to lose far more than a mere dwelling place:

> "For if the enemy takes his city, his altars are overturned, his fires are extinguished, his tombs are profaned, his temples are destroyed, and his worship is effaced"[4]

It is in this light that the ardent patriotism of the ancient Greek citizen may be most clearly grasped. Their piety, as we see, entailed a steadfast devotion to family, gods, and country, practically without distinction. One might reasonably assume, therefore,

---

1. Coulanges, *The Ancient City*   2. 218-19
3. Coulanges, *The Ancient City*   4. ibid.

that "it was almost impossible for private and public interests to conflict"[1] – almost, as Sophocles explores. For when the two interests are not aligned, which should take precedence, and who should be the arbiter? Among the city-states of the fifth century there were two prominent, contrasting examples in the form of Athens and Sparta, who ostensibly addressed the question rather differently, yet did so with many of the same underlying assumptions.

The rigid hierarchy, fervent militarism, and exacting discipline of Sparta's communitarian order presents an almost antithetical image to the democratic Athens of Pericles, which afforded "equal justice to all in their private differences" and where "the freedom which we enjoy in our government extends also to our ordinary life".[2] Yet both organised their societies with a view towards some notion of the common good. The relative degree of equality and liberty granted to the Athenian citizen vis-a-vis his Lacedæmonian cousin should not becloud the very real power both states exercised over their people.

Life, both private and public, was subject to the full purview of the state: an Athenian decree forbade men to remain single, while in Sparta both those who remained single and those who married late were punished. In Athens, idleness was made a crime for which the state could prescribe labour, while in Sparta,

---

1. ibid.   2. Thucydides, *The Peloponnesian War*, 2.37

pastimes and possessions deemed unnecessary or overindulgent were prohibited.[1] The enforcement of healthy social and cultural norms were central to the state's role, wherefore every aspect of a citizen's life was open to regulation. Education, in particular, was seen as paramount in forming responsible and capable citizens who could contribute positively to society. As two of Athens' most famous sons opined, "instruction for an end which is common should also itself be common. We must not regard a citizen as belonging just to himself; rather, we must regard every citizen as belonging to the city, since each is a part of the city"[2] and "the pupils shall be regarded as belonging to the state rather than to their parents".[3]

Political participation, meanwhile, was less a privilege than a duty in Athens, and failure to involve oneself in both the process and offices of governance could warrant a severe penalty. The same, again, for improper religious observance or neglect of the national festivals. This emphasis upon promotion of the common good limited the freedom of the individual, for better or worse, and instilled a collective spirit among the citizenry. As Aristotle believed, "the excellence of every part must be considered with regard to the excellence of the whole".[4]

---

1. Coulanges, *The Ancient City* 2. Aristotle, *Politics*, 1260b
3. Plato, *Laws*, VII 4. Aristotle, *Politics*, 1337a

The tension between individual liberty and the collective good was not likely to have been considered in such a social order, and, insofar as it was, would generally have been viewed as of little concern. A divergence between these interests will inevitably arise, of course, and in a society which perceived itself as just and open, as democratic Athens did, how was such a disharmony to be resolved? A cursory glance at history would suggest that it was invariably decided in favour of the state and the well-being of the country as a whole. Yet if there was to be an exception, it would surely be one which pertained to kinship and religion, the oldest and most profound of the three pillars of ancient identity.

The conflict with which we are confronted in *Antigone* thus derives from a society attempting to balance two strands of thought: a traditional order rooted in blood, ancestral custom, and the gods of the family hearth; and a civic order based around shared membership in the city-state, looser ties of kinship, staunch patriotism, and the gods of the polis. The former was governed by eternal law – believed to originate with the gods – while the latter was shaped increasingly by the edicts of men. In the dissonance between divine and mortal commandments, between family and fatherland, how was right to be defined, what form was justice to take, and what, if any, were to be the limits of the state's power over its citizens?

In approaching this question, Sophocles does not present us with an argument of abstractions; instead, the conflict is explored through the downfall of two quintessentially human characters. Their opposition is clear and absolute: Creon represents the duty of upholding order and obeying the laws of the state; Antigone, the duty of obeying the old laws of kinship and "listening to the private conscience".[1] Neither wishes, or is perhaps able, to consider the perspective of the other, and both act with unwavering resolution in their respective purposes. In the case of Antigone, at least, she is under no illusion that either will relent or that any understanding can be reached between them:

> "Then why delay? Your lecturing is pointless;
> every word repels me, and ever will it be thus,
> just as all that I speak must be odious to you"[2]

They are indeed equally headstrong, and though a fatal flaw for both characters, their single-mindedness gives voice to each position without compromise. Furthermore, by having Antigone err and Creon speak to his beliefs with sound reasoning, we are compelled to give due consideration to both positions: "Sophocles allows Creon to put his case ably, and, in a measure from which an inferior artist

---

1. Richard Jebb, *Antigone*   2. 565-7

might have shrunk, he was content to make Antigone merely a nobly heroic woman, not a being exempt from human passion and human weakness"[1]

While modern audiences may be inclined to see a clear division between right and wrong, with Antigone the sympathetic heroine and Creon the unsympathetic villain, it is worth considering that a contemporary Greek audience would have regarded the play and its central figures somewhat differently, especially during the opening stages.

From his introduction, Creon is presented as the model of rulership during a time of crisis: he has successfully steered the city away from disaster and committed himself as the rightful successor to placing the safety and well-being of Thebes above all else. His opening speech on just rulership and the principles which govern a healthy and upright society will have been eminently agreeable to an ancient audience, most pertinently his insistence that loyalty to the city must take precedence over any private relationship:

> "any man who would place a friend
> above the good of his own fatherland,
> that man, I say, is beneath regard.
> May Zeus be my witness, he who sees all, always:
> never would I stand idly by if ruin I saw
> marching upon the people, their safety in doubt;

---

[1]. Jebb, *Antigone*

> nor would I ever make a friend of one
> who threatened to bring our country low.
> For this I know well: the city is our home,
> our deliverance, our prosperity,
> and only when she sails straight and true
> may the bonds of real brotherhood be formed"[1]

Creon's arguments are delivered eloquently and appeal to commonly held sentiments. Indeed, the highly esteemed fourth century orator and statesman, Demosthenes, employed Creon's opening speech in court so as to illustrate the proper conduct befitting a citizen.[2] Any misgivings among the audience – or the play's chorus – upon hearing of Polynikes' punishment are thus somewhat tempered. The exposure of a corpse was a terrible act, but equally, few crimes were considered more deplorable than the betrayal of one's own fatherland. As Hegel remarked, the "proclamation was so far justifiable in that it expressed care for the welfare of the entire city".[3] The matter-of-fact response from the chorus to Creon's edict certainly suggests more than a hint of reservation, however, and we may assume that this was shared by the audience, for Hellenic society did not treat lightly the denial of sepulture.

The ancient Greeks held burial and performance of the attendant rites to be a sacred obligation of the

---

1. 210-221   2. Demosthenes, *On the False Embassy*
3. Hegel, *The Philosophy of Fine Art*

utmost import. Without them, it was believed that the soul of the deceased could obtain no rest in the world below. For so long as the body remained unburied, the spirits of the dead would be left to wander, deprived of the repose each sought in vain at life's end. Consequently, "men feared death less than the privation of burial, for rest and eternal happiness were at stake".[1] The unwritten laws of Greek warfare attest to this belief: after a battle, it was customary to agree a truce for the removal of the dead; conquerors were expected to allow the vanquished to bury their fallen, and if the latter were unable to fulfil this duty, the responsibility fell upon the victors. Nor was this practice limited to fellow Hellenes, as evinced when the invading Persians slain at Marathon were buried by the Athenians.

In the Iliad, Homer presents us with a harrowing illustration of the significance of burial rites when Achilles, consumed with wrath at the death of his close friend, Patroclus, confronts the Trojan prince, Hektor, outside the gates of Troy. Hektor, the slayer of Patroclus, swears before the gods that if he should emerge victorious, he shall return Achilles' body to his countrymen; he asks only that he be afforded the same grace should he be defeated. The vengeful Achæan refuses. With the contest subsequently decided in favour of Achilles, the mortally wounded

---

[1]. Coulanges, *The Ancient City*

Hektor appeals to his enemy one last time:

> "I beg you, by your soul and by your parents,
> do not let the dogs devour me by your ships.
> Accept the ransom of bronze and gold, the gifts
> my father, and her ladyship my mother, will provide.
> Let them have my body back, let them carry me home
> so that our men and women may accord me
> the fitting rites of fire when I am dead"[1]

Yet still Achilles remains unmoved. He is gripped in the fury of battle, the anguish of his loss, and can only respond with the grim promise that "the dogs and birds will feast on you, blood and bone!"[2] With his last words, Hektor calls down a curse upon Achilles, foretelling that, for drawing the gods' wrath, that day will come when "Paris and lord Apollo destroy you at the Gates".[3] Achilles, unrelenting, ties Hektor's corpse to the back of his chariot, dragging it along the ground as he rides first around the walls of Troy, then back to the Achæan encampment, trampling upon the laws that separate the civilised and the barbaric, the pious and the impious. After his return, he circles the funeral pyre of Patroclus repeatedly, the body still trailing through the dust in his wake.

Mercifully, and in a clear expression of the Greek sentiment, the gods intervene: Apollo places his divine

---

1. *The Iliad*, XXII, 338-44   2. ibid., 354   3. ibid., XX, 358-60

shield over Hektor's corpse, protecting it from the ravages of its desecration. After the gods have taken counsel, Zeus decrees that Achilles must release the body to Hektor's father, Priam, who shall go in person to recover his son's remains. What follows is a passage of unparalleled beauty in which the aged king of Troy comes to the tent of Achilles, alone and defenceless, at the mercy of his enemy, to beseech the return of his son's body. The warrior who has lost his closest friend and the king who has lost his son and heir share in a moment of reconciliation, the compassion of man for man emerging, if briefly, from the devastation of a long and bitter war. Achilles' wrath at last subsides and Hektor, returned to his family, is duly honoured with all rites in a fitting burial.

To deny sepulture to the dead, especially in war, was exceptionally rare. The most notable example comes from the Peloponnesian War when, at the decisive battle of Ægospotami, the Spartan general Lysander put some four thousand Athenian captives to death and then refused them burial – an act which blackened his name in the annals of classical history.[1]

Away from the battlefield, the picture is somewhat less clear. It is generally accepted that traitors would be denied burial on their native soil, and that privation of sepulture was historically one of the punishments that could be imposed upon those found guilty of the

---
1. Pausanias, 9.32.9

most severe crimes. How often this occurred, however, is questionable. Thus, while Creon's edict was not without some precedent, it will have assuredly filled most Greeks with a considerable degree of unease.

When the play opens and we are introduced to Antigone for the first time, she is understandably distraught: both her brothers have been slain in war – at the hands of the other, no less – and now she learns that one of them, Polynikes, is to be denied burial, left as "carrion for the dogs and birds to tear at".[1] She deplores the proclamation and feels personally targeted – "such is the law that our good king Creon decrees for you and me – for me, Ismene!"[2] – as indeed she might, for in Greece, women played a significant role in the funeral rites, and as the only remaining members of the house of Oedipus, it is the two sisters who would have borne this sacred duty. That Antigone singles herself out in the presence of Ismene may be excused in that she appears to shoulder the greater responsibility.

In this opening exchange, we see the fiery nature of Antigone, the wild passion that will emerge time and again throughout the play. To her, the obligations of kinship are paramount; all other concerns are not merely secondary, but inconsequential. She cannot image that Ismene would feel otherwise, and at the slightest hint of hesitancy, she turns on her sister,

---

1. 240   2. 39

scorning her: "nor if your heart should come to change will I welcome your help; your hands, if willing, will not labour with mine".[1] When it becomes clear that Ismene does not wish to disobey the order, her language becomes almost contemptuous: "if you truly mean what you say, my hatred you will have".[2]

Ismene, for her part, should not be misunderstood, nor brandished a coward outright for her reluctance. Upon hearing of the edict and her sister's intentions, she is asked – expected, rather – to defy the state and incur the punishment of death, a fate that her only remaining relative is intent on pursuing with or without her. Ismene is conscious of the power of the state; she feels that any attempt to bury Polynikes would be futile as Creon's guards might immediately expose the body once more, if indeed the rites could be performed at all. Antigone is either blind to this consideration or simply undeterred by it. Thus, when Antigone accuses her of disregarding the laws which the gods hold in honour, Ismene responds, no doubt truthfully, "dishonour them I do not, yet nor have I the strength to defy the city, to oppose the will of the king".[3]

In this we may understand the difference between the two sisters: Ismene is a citizen like any other, "a beautiful standard of the commonplace",[4] and as such should not be judged by the exceptional heights of

---

1. 88-9   2. 116-7   3. 98-9   4. Goethe, *Conversations*

Antigone's heroism. She has not the will to face death in pursuit of an "impossible" deed; she sees her sister's actions as futile, and is unable to understand why she would throw her life away, whereas Antigone is prepared to act in spite of that potential futility.

Ismene's attempts to dissuade her sister fall on deaf ears: she recounts the long line of tragedies that have befallen their family, eager to prevent yet another, but to no avail. In this, for as much as she may pale beside Antigone's burning devotion, we may have sympathy for her. She has not the strength of her sister, but she is no less loving, as her final words to the departing Antigone show: "then go, if go you must, but please know this: however reckless your path, to the ones who love you, you are – and always will be – truly dear".[1]

When Antigone is subsequently brought before Creon – to the disbelief of all – he is met not with denial, nor obfuscation, nor pleading, but defiance: "I admit it. I do not deny a thing".[2] In the exchange that follows, the conflict between the two antagonists is defined clearly and unequivocally; they speak to two different ideals with no thought of compromise. Creon refers only to the law of the state, the authority of the king, while Antigone defers to eternal law and the supremacy of the gods – "it was not Zeus who decreed it, the Father of All did not command this of me".[3]

---

1. 121-23   2. 502   3. 509-10

In questioning her decision to honour Polynikes, an enemy of Thebes, Creon appeals to the loyalty of each citizen to the state and the brotherhood of the polis, while Antigone thinks only of the bond of kinship and the duty to one's family, irrespective of the political implications. In a perfect encapsulation of their contrasting values, Creon asks how she can honour both brothers with the same rites when one perished nobly in defence of Thebes, and the other led a foreign army against their city and died a traitor, to which Antigone merely responds: "death is death just the same, and Hades expects, demands these rites for all".[1]

Her refusal to yield is an affront to Creon. He perceives her recalcitrance, and the act itself, as being done expressly to undermine his rule. As his frustration with Antigone grows to the point of anger, he calls for Ismene to be brought forth from the royal house, accusing her of complicity in her sister's deed – "if only I had known I was nurturing twin afflictions, two rebels against my throne".[2] With a final affirmation that Antigone is to be executed, both sisters are led away under guard, leaving the audience to reflect upon the arguments made.

In the dissension between Creon and Antigone, we see both characters place a strong emphasis upon law. Insofar as one may be definitively right and the

---

1. 590-92   2. 606-8

other wrong, the appeal to law demonstrates a belief in objective justice, traditionally understood to be overseen by the gods. Indeed, law itself, eternal and divine, was given to man by the gods: "the Cretans attributed their laws not to Minos, but to Zeus; the Lacedæmonians believed that their legislator was not Lycurgus, but Apollo; the Romans believed that Numa wrote under the dictation of one of the most powerful divinities of ancient Italy – the goddess Egeria; and the Etruscans received their laws from the god Tages"[1]

All law, from the traditional customs practised among individuals, families, and tribes for countless generations, to the edicts promulgated by political states, was understood to either derive from or at the very least be in accordance with the original law. In the case of the latter, legislators would often consult with religious figures and perform the necessary rites to ensure that a decree was in harmony with divine law, much of which was unwritten and effectively timeless. It was for this reason that Heraclitus remarked how "all human laws are in the keeping of the one divine law",[2] and Plato proclaimed that to obey the laws is to obey the gods.[3] Alongside and very much in association with the law as most understand it today – that is to say, a collection of proscriptions

---

1. Coulanges, *The Ancient City* 2. Heraclitus, fr. 114
3. Coulanges, *The Ancient City*

and less commonly prescriptions which govern a social order – the ancients believed in a higher law which in a "very potent way affected and controlled the destinies of men".[1] Thus we may understand Antigone when she dismisses the significance of Creon's edict:

> "nor did I believe your word held such force
> that you, a mortal, could overrule the gods,
> the unwritten and unfailing, immutable laws.
> For their life is not merely of this day or the last,
> but for all time, a tradition rooted in the dawn,
> and no one knows when they first saw light"[2]

If Antigone is in open rebellion against the king, she does so in deference to a higher authority, that of the gods, and by defying his law, she upholds and defends theirs. In turn, though perhaps unwittingly as we shall discuss, Creon acts in defiance of the gods, overriding the very laws which they hold in honour and thereby sowing the seeds of his eventual downfall. For "those laws resting on unwritten custom are yet more sovereign, and concerned with issues of still more sovereign importance, than written laws".[3]

We should not think, however, that Creon is an impious man – far from it. His gods are the gods of Thebes, of the city that houses their temples and shrines, honours them with public offerings, and celebrates them

---

[1]. James Beck, *The Higher Law*   [2]. 513-18   [3]. Aristotle, *Politics*, 1287b

in national festivals. In his initial proclamation and speech, we may believe that he is sincerely devoted to the polis and its religious institutions. Creon attributes the city's preservation to the gods, and forbids the burial of Polynikes for the express reason that he "returned to the home of his fathers and the gods of his people" at the head of a foreign army, "desiring above all with a most violent passion to burn the city from temple to hearth"[1] – a fact which Antigone never disputes, or even acknowledges. Furthermore, when the chorus later suggest that the burial of Polynikes may have been an intervention by the gods, Creon's rebuttal is quite definitive:

> "it is absurd – egregious – to suggest that the gods
> would have the slightest concern for that corpse!
> Tell me, was it in honour of his noble deeds,
> his piety, that they sought to bury him? The exile
> who returned to burn their pillared temples,
> to set their sacred shrines aflame, to reduce
> their hallowed land to ash, and scatter its laws
> to the winds? Do you truly believe that the gods
> would hold such a man in high regard? That they
> would honour such treachery? Unthinkable!"[2]

Again, we may safely assume that many, perhaps most, of Sophocles' contemporary audience would have concurred with Creon in this. His arguments are

---

1. 232-5   3. 333-42

based in an absolute patriotism which, as we have discussed, was itself bound up with religion. The respective positions of Creon and Antigone, then, are compelling enough to divide the sympathies of the audience. Both appear pious in their own right; both hold steadfast to the law and the loyalty which they regard as foremost. And yet the favourable impression given of Creon in his opening speech fades over the course of the play. Any unease felt towards the punishment of Polynikes gradually extends to the man himself, with mounting reservations about his temper and conduct as king. As Creon himself admits, "it is impossible to know a man truly, his character, his mind, his sense of judgement, till he has proved himself in the task of ruling, his command of the law – the test of kingship",[1] and in each he falls short.

The denial of burial to Polynikes sets the events of the play in motion, and everything that transpires follows from this decision – a decision which, as we learn, Creon took without consulting Tiresias and by extension the gods. It is the first and most fatal of the king's misjudgements. During the Argive invasion, Creon sought and duly heeded the counsel of Tiresias, and as a result the city was saved from destruction. When the two meet again towards the end of the play, the blind seer is quick to remind him of this, and Creon happily concurs – "experience has

---

1. 201-203

shown me your wisdom".[1] In this light, his failure to speak with the old prophet before pronouncing his edict is all the more questionable. One could interpret this as mere oversight: the war had only just ended and Creon, newly enthroned, was very much occupied with steadying the ship of state. Alternatively, it could be attributed to the self-assurance, or even arrogance, of a new king wishing to impose his authority on the first day of his reign. Creon, it may be suggested, was utterly convinced of the righteousness of his own actions, certain that he enjoyed the assent of the gods, and thus saw no need to seek the counsel of a seer. One is certainly more damning than the other, and as the play bears out, there is little reason not to believe in the latter.

Throughout the play, most notably in his discussions with Hæmon and Tiresias, Creon takes great exception to anyone who dares to call his judgement into question. Even the slightest dissent is met with immediate and unbridled invective. When his son tentatively attempts to address the subject – "I am neither able, nor in truth do I wish, to say how your words may be wrong. Perhaps, however, there are others who could, whose thoughts we might find to be of use"[2] – he is dismissed out of hand on account of his age. Hæmon urges his father to consider the counsel of those with worthy advice, to respect the

---

[1]. 1123   [2]. 790

gods of the hearth and the kindred rites they honour, wherefore he is simply brandished a "pathetic child" and "an utter wretch".[1] Once more, when Tiresias, the highly respected seer who by Creon's own admission has helped him in the past, informs the king of the terrible omen he has witnessed, the failure of the offering, how the flesh of Polynikes' corpse has defiled the shrines and temples, he is unmoved. He reviles Tiresias and his fellow seers as a "coin-clutching tribe of fortune-tellers",[2] accusing him of being blinded by his "love of injustice".[3] Even in these exchanges, most especially his comments concerning the importance of order and the dangers of anarchy, Creon offers sound arguments which demand consideration. And yet, by dismissing any and all disagreement, disregarding the counsel of people close to him, and vilifying those who seek to help him, including his own son, he ensures his own doom. Any sympathy the audience would have harboured for him and his position are quickly dissipated as his wrathful and obstinate conduct worsens – two traits that would have been recognised, particularly among an Athenian audience, as markers of tyranny.

To understand the ideal model of kingship in the ancient Greek world, we may refer as ever to Homer. Firstly, the singular authority of the king as an emulation of the pantheon, legitimised by the father

---

1. 859   2. 1177   3. 1211

of all, Zeus himself:

> "how can all Achæans be masters here in Troy?
> Too many kings will ruin an army – mob rule!
> Let there be one commander, one master only,
> endowed by Zeus, son of crooked-minded Kronos,
> with kingly sceptre and royal rights of custom"[1]

The ideal king is not envisioned as a tyrant, however. He is expected to welcome dissent, seek out counsel, and even tolerate a degree of effrontery from his peers.[2] We see this dynamic instanced in another scene from the Iliad in which lord Agamemnon proposes to his disconsolate troops – the tide of battle having turned against the Achæans – that they concede defeat and flee back across the Ægean. At this suggestion, one among the ranks, Diomedes, steps forward to contend with the king – "I will be the first to oppose you in your folly, here in assembly, where it is the custom".[3]

Creon's refusal to entertain criticism, however mild or well-reasoned, is thus arguably his greatest failing as a king. By refusing all counsel and disdaining the views of others, he comes to recognise his error too late. He considers himself equal to the polis – "has the city not always belonged to he who rules?"[4] – and his judgement equal to the *nomos*, the law.[5] This is

---

1. *The Iliad*, II, 235-9   2. Durocher, *The Ancient Ethnostate*
3. *The Iliad*, IX, 36-7   4. 848   5. Karl Reinhardt, *Sophocles*

demonstrated most explicitly in the conversation with his son. When Hæmon explains to his father that the people of Thebes are appalled by the impending execution of Antigone – "no woman", they say, "ever deserved death less, the worst of punishments for the most noble of deeds"[1] – and that an outcry against his rule is spreading amongst the citizenry, Creon is indifferent. He asks Hæmon, almost rhetorically, "is the city to dictate how I rule?".[2] Such disdain for his fellow Thebans, while doubtless offensive to the sensibilities of a democratic Athenian, would not reflect well on a king in the Homeric Age either, as we have discussed. If the exchange with Hæmon displays his hubris in the sight of men, then the following with Tiresias brings to the fore his hubris in the sight of the gods.[3]

The old seer explains to Creon that every public altar and hearth in the city has been "sullied, defiled by the birds and dogs with carrion, foul flesh torn from the fallen son of Oedipus", and as a consequence the gods no longer accept their prayers – they have become "cold to our flame, our burnt-offerings".[4] He implores him to relent and reconsider his judgement, conscious of the fate which awaits both the king and the city. Once more, Creon rejects the counsel which is offered, disparaging Tiresias as a mere profit-seeker who wishes to undermine his nascent rule for material gain.

---

1. 898-9   2. 844   3. Reinhardt, *Sophocles*   4. 1152-6

Worse still, in vowing that the edict shall be upheld and the remains of Polynikes left unburied, he blasphemes against the gods:

> "not even if the eagles of Zeus himself
> should tear at the corpse, snatch up the rotting flesh
> and wing their spoils away, up to Olympus,
> gorging themselves beside his high throne.
>
>   No,
> not even then, not for fear of such defilement
> would I allow that traitor to be buried"[1]

Creon's immediate justification for these words, his belief that "no mortal has the power to defile the gods",[2] rings hollow. Confronted with such obstinacy, insolence, and impiety, Tiresias delivers his final speech, a prophecy of the doom which Creon has invited upon himself. Death shall soon befall his house; the neighbouring cities shall rise up against him; and now, "the grim Furies, fell daughters of Night" lie in wait for him, "the avenging Erinyes sent forth by Hades and the high gods"[3] to visit upon him the very misery he has caused. Blood for blood; two lives taken, those of his son and his wife, for the life he has "wrongly entombed" and the life he has kept from the world below. Tiresias' revealed omen carries the weight of a curse, and at last, with the fear of loss and the wrath of the gods upon him, Creon realises

---

1. 1184-89   2. 1190-91   3. 1231-33

his misjudgement. And yet, it is too late. The words of Tiresias will all come to pass, for his downfall is already sealed.

The Greeks believed in a "higher law of retributive justice, eternal, immutable"[1] from whose workings no man could escape, and the Erinyes, or Furies, were often the pitiless agents of this law, bringing to justice those who had offended the sacred ordinances, especially those pertaining to bonds of kinship. That Creon should have suffered divine punishment is far from surprising when one considers his actions: he profanes the gods of the underworld by withholding a soul that by rights should be with them, and profanes the gods of Olympus by exposing a corpse to the heavens and allowing its decaying flesh to sully their altars. With respect to the latter, it should be understood that, for the Greeks, particularly in the Homeric vision of the divine, there was a sharp division between the world of the dead and the world of the living, between Hades and Olympus, between the cthonic gods of the underworld and the blissful gods of the heavens. For the Olympians, death was, with rare exception, something wholly divorced from their existence, such that they would not, or could not, come into contact with the dead. In Euripides, for instance, the goddess Artemis is unable to remain beside her favourite, Hippolytus, because his death

---

1. Beck, *The Higher Law*

approaches: "farewell, for I may not look upon the dead, nor defile my sight with the anguish of departing breath, and I see that you are already near life's end".[1] Such was the outrage he forces upon the gods, punishing in turn the very person who sought to rectify his sacrilege.

Creon errs in that he commits himself entirely to the supremacy of the polis, with no thought for the familial or the individual. In his efforts to unify the city, maintain order, and reaffirm the duties of each citizen to the broader community, he tramples upon the time-honoured customs concerning kinship and death. "The intrinsically sound maxims of government upon which he relies lose all validity when opposed to the higher law"[2] which he was disregarding. For while the gods may indeed despise a traitor, no less do they despise the impious:

> "Zeus pours down his pelting, punishing rains,
> wrathful, furious, storming against those men
> who enforce their crooked judgements
> and banish justice from the city
> with no regard for the vengeance of the gods"[3]

Creon's ruination comes to pass not because of a single act of impiety or misjudgement, but rather an unshakeable imprudence that drives him inexorably to his downfall. At his lowest moment, when the scale of

---

1. Eurip., *Hippolytus*, 1436-9   2. Jebb, *Antigone*   3. *Iliad*, XVI, 457-61

his folly is made clear to him, he desperately wonders if some god had struck him blind, "a mighty blow that robbed me of my senses, driving me down wild and ruinous paths".[1] However literally we may wish to interpret this expression, it was certainly a common sentiment among the Greeks. As the ancient proverb went, "those whom the gods wish to destroy, they first confound the mind". Sophocles himself was no doubt in agreement with this, for immediately after Antigone has been sentenced to death, and just moments before the confrontation with Hæmon, the Chorus sings in the presence of Creon:

> *"Wise, indeed, was the one who first spoke*
> *that famous saying: 'sooner or later,*
> *evil will seem good, good will seem evil*
> *to him whose mind the gods lead to ruin'.*
> *For only the briefest, most fleeting of moments*
> *will he fare free before meeting his doom"*[2]

The bitterness of Creon and Antigone's conflict is driven primarily, as we have seen, by the single-mindedness of the two characters: they are fuel to each other's flame, each as steadfast in their belief as the other, so much so that Reinhardt described the play as "two types of blindness"[3] confronting one another. What, then, distinguishes them; why is our sympathy naturally drawn to Antigone? In a mirror image of

---

1. 1460-1   2. 710-15   3. Reinhardt, *Sophocles*

Creon's neglect of the domestic, Antigone gives little heed, or indeed none, to the privileges conferred and duties imposed by membership of the polis, nor the significance of a social body above – or at least of equal weight to – the family. The gods of the city are relegated below those of the domestic hearth, and at no point does she acknowledge Polynikes' role in the Argive invasion of her homeland. The answer, it may be suggested, is one of motivation.

Creon's decree, though not wholly without justification, is a principally political action, one that demands nothing of him in its fulfilment and reflects a less than noble temper. For in the words of Homer, by punishing the dead, he stabs at a man who is already down, and as Tiresias remarks, "what glory can be won, what valour is there in slaying the dead again?".[1] Given the contrast with Antigone, as we shall discuss, his entrenchment – in defence, it seems, of his own authority more so than any higher principle – could be viewed as mere stubbornness born out of pride. Antigone, conversely, is animated by an ethic of equal sovereignty, but greater nobility, which is the unconditional love for and devotion to her brother. She cannot bear to see his body left unburied, to become carrion for the feral dogs and birds, for "to leave such a duty unfulfilled would be in direct opposition to the sacred commitments of her

---

1. 1170-71

personal relationship".[1] Her defiance, however single-minded, is in service of a piety for which she is prepared to give her life. Thus we find ourselves not merely inclined to forgive her intemperance, her disregard for the broader political context of her actions, but to celebrate her.

In Antigone's final appearance, as the guards slowly, and one might suggest reluctantly, lead her to her tomb beyond the city walls, she demands the attention of the Theban elders. Although at no point in the play does the chorus explicitly defend Antigone or support her actions, the sight of her being led to her death moves them to sympathy. They wonder if she suffers still for the woes of Oedipus, the outrage that brought her into being, and Antigone is left to ponder the same – "a union cursed, and I its wretched child".[2] The dreadful chain of tragedies that has befallen the line of Laius leaves Antigone clinging to a familial bond that, in the world of the living at least, is all but gone. She is unable or unwilling to recognise the severity of Polynikes' crime precisely because of this, and amidst the endless misery afflicting her family, she can do nothing but remain steadfast in her duties and unwavering in her loyalty to her disgraced brother, just as she had done for her disgraced father.

Antigone recounts how she performed the burial rites for her mother, father, and Eteocles, almost

---

1. Hegel, *The Philosophy of Fine Art*   2. 982-3

appealing, it seems, to her departed kin: "when you perished I tended to your bodies, washed and adorned them with my own hands, poured sweet libations upon your graves".[1] She then asks, perhaps of the chorus, perhaps of the gods, why she is to be punished for carrying out the same duty for Polynikes. As was the traditional belief, the family for Antigone is not merely a natural, but a sacred institution, one honoured by the gods and supported by an eternal law that was enforced by Zeus, Dikē, and the other gods.[2] And yet, for abiding by these very laws, she finds herself being led to the rocky chamber which is to serve as her tomb. Understandably, she begins to question the righteousness of her actions, and for the first time doubt creeps into her words.

What follows is by far the most contentious passage in the whole play. The German poet Goethe took such exception to the verses in question that he hoped they might be proven a foreign addition to Sophocles' original work: "there is a passage in *Antigone* which I always look upon as a blemish, and I would give a great deal for a skilled philologist to prove that it is interpolated and spurious".[3] The offending lines are indeed curious. After speaking admirably to her conviction and standing resolutely by her deed – "I honoured you, as was right, as the

---

1. 1016-18   2. Ahrensdorf, *Greek Tragedy and Political Philosophy*
3. Goethe, *Conversations*

pious, the wise, the honest all know"[1] – she proceeds to offer an additional justification:

> "if, in truth, I had been the mother of children,
> or if a husband in death had been left unburied,
> never would I have defied the will of our people,
> never taken this hardship upon myself.
> By reason of what law, you ask, do I say this?
> Were my husband to die, I might find another,
> and if a child were lost, we could bear yet more.
> But with mother and father both lost to Hades,
> no brother could ever be brought forth again"[2]

There is certainly a line of reasoning to this argument, yet it is one wholly unbecoming of Antigone's final speech. The loftiness of her intent, the unyielding commitment to her kin and the time-honoured customs of blood and hearth, the laws sacred to the gods, upheld staunchly before the promise of death, is reduced to what seems a cold and mundane calculation bereft of the spirit which has driven her throughout the play.

What makes these lines all the more curious is that they clearly echo a passage found in Herodotus in which a Persian woman, the wife of Intaphrenes, is told she may save one member of her family. She elects to save the life of her brother rather than her husband or children, and when, at the request of the

---
1. 1021-22   2. 1023-31

king, Darius, she is asked why, her response is as follows: "god willing, I may have another husband, and other children when these are gone. But as my father and mother are both dead, I can never possibly have another brother. That was the reason for what I said".[1] This story, like many in Herodotus, relates the experience of an individual who is forced to choose between extreme imperatives, such as duty to kin and state when the two are in conflict.[2] We may understand, then, why Sophocles was inspired to refer to it, if indeed he did. Since the brother of Intaphrenes' wife was still alive, however, the decision to choose her closest kin and place the duty towards her ancestral line first is perfectly coherent. In the case of Antigone, by contrast, the same reasoning does not apply for it is a question of burial rites, not the preservation of life, nor is she confronted with such a choice. Furthermore, by suggesting that she would not defy the state and risk her life for the sake of a loving husband or her own children, these verses somewhat tarnish, if but for a moment, the clear purity of her purpose.

If we are to accept the authenticity of this passage, as seems probable given its inclusion, without contention, in the commentary of Aristotle, then we may alleviate its incongruity with the following consideration: these verses come during Antigone's

---

1. Herodotus, 3.119.6   2. Durocher, *The Ancient Ethnostate*

only period of self-doubt; in seeking to reassure herself and convince the chorus of the lawfulness of her deed, she appeals to the oldest and most revered ordinances which constitute the bonds of blood and kinship – the duty of children to parents, and of sibling to sibling. As portrayed in the story of Althæa and Meleager, in which the queen of Calydon commits her own son to destruction because he had taken the life of her brother, a clear hierarchy of familial obligation existed, and it is to this that Antigone speaks, however harsh or improper it may sound to our ears.

With her belief shaken, she calls out to any who might assuage her doubt, pleading to know why the gods appear silent, "O tell me, what sacred law have I transgressed? Why in my despair should I still look to the gods?".[1] And yet this uncertainty, spurred by the imminence of her entombment and the fear that she hasn't the favour of the gods, does not deter her: she has laid bare the agonies of her soul and emerged with undiminished resolve – "still the same tempest, the same fierce passion raging in her soul".[2] She yields nothing; there is no tempering of her conviction, no appeal for mercy at the final hour. Antigone accepts her fate and only demands of the gods that, should she be righteous in her actions, they mete out justice on her behalf: "if they are wrong, if my judges have erred, may they suffer no less, may their punishment

---

1. 1040-41   2. 1051

befit the injustice they impose upon me!"[1] In her final words, she calls upon "fair Thebes, city of my fathers"[2] to behold her doom, and affirms one last time that she goes to her death, without regret or reservation, in defence of divine law and the sacred bonds of kinship, condemned to an early grave for "piety, for devotion, my reverence for the gods!"[3]

With this parting speech, Antigone is led away to be entombed alive, no funeral dirge or weeping of loved ones to accompany her burial. When we see her next, death has already claimed her; she has taken her own life, hanged herself in a noose woven from her veil. In this final act, one may reasonably perceive an element of despair, the realisation that no one, no god or loved one, would be coming; that she had found herself alone – truly alone – abandoned to endure a prolonged and miserable death, with nothing to dispel the creeping doubt that perhaps she had been in the wrong throughout, and that justice lay not with her but with her persecutors. For in her own words, if the gods approve of her punishment, of the "criminal's fate",[4] then there would be nothing for it but to abide by their judgement: "once I have suffered, I will know that I was wrong, and with that I shall gladly accept my doom".[5]

Why, then, do the gods not intervene to save her? Why is she left to take her own life, possibly in the

---

1. 1048-50   2. 1057   3. 1063-4   4. 1044   5. 1046-47

belief that her actions were misguided? The play itself provides no clear answer. Instead, we have only to consider perhaps the most persistent theme of ancient literature, the very doom to which Antigone submits, the eternal and all-pervasive, "unknowable but certain"[1] fate, a power to which even the gods were subject: "death is certain, and when a man's fate has come, not even the gods can save him, no matter how they may love him".[2] We see, then, that Antigone's suffering needn't be viewed as a sign of disfavour from the gods. For as Schiller wrote of Achilles:

"nor did his immortal mother save the hero divine"[3]

The profound power of fate is "fathomless",[4] so speak the Chorus, while the workings of the divine are, according to Sophocles himself, beyond the reckoning of man.[5] So it is that Antigone's death is transformed from tragedy into triumph. Creon's realisation, miraculous as we might describe it, occurs in all probability after she has met her end, whereupon Polynikes is at last given a fitting burial, and the king is made to suffer complete and utter devastation. In this light, Antigone's parting invocation to the gods, her plea for Creon to be punished, takes on the quality of a pact, one that could only be fulfilled

---

1. Heaney, *Beowulf* 2. *The Odyssey*, III, 236 3. Schiller, *Nänie*
4. 1074 5. Sophocles, fr. 919

with her passing. By taking her own life, she ensures both the downfall of Creon and the burial of her brother, wherein death becomes the final expression of her defiance.

When Creon, seeking to right the wrongs of his brief rule, comes upon the corpse of Antigone, he finds Hæmon knelt beside her, grieving desperately, "his trembling arms wrapped about her waist".[1] At once, with the words of Tiresias doubtless haunting his thoughts, Creon calls out in a panic – "come out, my son, come now, I beg of you!"[2] – yet Hæmon, inconsolable for the loss of his bride, is filled only with resentment and rage at the sight of his father, the cause, as he sees it, of this grim misery. Without a word, he draws his sword and lunges at Creon, failing to land the blow. Overcome by grief – and we may assume shame at the attempted murder of his father – he immediately turns the blade on himself and buries it deep into his body. The attack on Creon renders Hæmon's suicide all the more disquieting, particularly for an ancient audience. It is the only example in classical Greek literature of a character intentionally attempting to commit patricide, an act so abominable that when Oedipus discovers he has taken the life of his own father, albeit unknowingly, his self-condemnation is absolute: "what is left to say? I must perish, the parricide, unholy anathema that I am".[3]

---

1. 1400   2. 1409   3. *Oedipus Tyrannus*, 1440

The first devastation for Creon, then, is the loss of his last living son, just as Tiresias had foretold. For the Greeks, the fortunes of one's descendants was of paramount importance and central to the happiness of each,[1] wherefore the gods were said to punish the impious by rendering their lineage barren.[2] While the loss of any child is awful, the loss of one's only remaining child is thus even more severe, for "it signifies the end of one's lineage, of one's flesh and blood, and therefore, in some sense, of one's self"[3] – a sentiment that Creon himself comes to express before the play's end.

While the omen spoken by Tiresias moved Creon to relent and reverse his judgements, the death of Hæmon elicits severe self-reproach and the bearing of guilt for all that has transpired:

"curse the misdeeds of unthinking minds,
senseless and stubborn, yielding only death!
O men of Thebes, look upon us, behold,
two kinsmen, flesh and blood, killer and killed!
What misery born of my laws, my words...
O my child, my dear son, gone, dead so young!
You depart this world, your life cut short,
not by your own foolishness, but by mine"[4]

---

1. Aristotle, *Nico. Ethics*, 1.11   2. Durocher, *Ancient Ethnostate*
3. Ahrensdorf, *Greek Tragedy and Political Philosophy*   4. 1050-57

His remorseful confession is swiftly followed by the second devastation, the suicide of Eurydice. The messenger returns and informs Creon of his wife's death, how "with her dying breath she called down torments upon"[1] him, holding him to blame for the doom of their sons. With this final blow, his ruin is complete; he calls out to the gods "I can fall no further, I have sunk to the very depths of woe",[2] and wishes only to be led away, to sink into oblivion. He has lost all that is dear to him, all that gives meaning and joy to his life, and in Sophocles' own words, "when a man has lost his joys, he lives not, but lasts, a corpse that still draws breath".[3] Before our eyes, Creon dwindles into nothingness – "I who live no more, who am less than nothing".[4] He begs for the agony to end, praying to the gods for death, for "that finest fate of all",[5] his final day, yet no such relief is forthcoming. For Creon, life is to be his punishment, just as death was Antigone's reward.

Of the many themes presented in the play, we may venture to draw a few conclusions from its resolution. In the downfall of Creon we see the folly of man's hubris in presuming or overruling the will of the gods, or, more broadly, the notion that "all men and all political institutions are ultimately subordinate to the operations of the higher law", and that violation of this law, knowingly or otherwise, invites retributive

---

1. 1491-1   2. 1496-7   3. 1330-31   4. 1509   5. 1514

justice.[1] While this much is quite clear, Sophocles' treatment of the tangled conflict between kin and country is somewhat less unequivocal. Creon's exhortations to collective loyalty and duty to the city go unchallenged – save for his more tyrannical and self-serving utterances – and are presented in a very compelling light. What may be said, and is made explicit by Creon's own admission – "it is best to observe the old laws passed down to us always and ever, to the very day we die"[2] – is that devotion to the family must be respected in matters of religious custom and similar duties of kinship, irrespective of political considerations. The bonds of blood are evidently sacred and must never be disregarded by the state, for a healthy society is held together not merely by the common loyalty of all to the state and its legitimate representatives, but by powerful familial and religious sentiments.[3]

Beyond these overarching ideas, we may admire the very Sophoclean theme of individual will, of the character who holds to their conscience, refusing to submit and thus going to their deaths unbowed, unrepentant, triumphant in their defiance. Of this, Antigone is perhaps the crowning example. In her contravention of Creon's edict there is no hesitation, no thought of compromise or submission; the duty to her brother is sacrosanct and no one, not Ismene, not

---

[1] Beck, *The Higher Law*   [2] 1280-82   [3] Durocher, *The Anc. Ethno.*

the king himself, can dissuade or deter her from fulfilling the commitment which she believes to be just. Those who oppose her are met only with disdain, while even her own sister is briefly vilified for having sought to discourage her. This blind will, as the Chorus reminds her,[1] is what destroys her, and yet it is this same vital, unyielding spirit, this heroic temper that ennobles her and ultimately ensures that her sacred duty is observed. This conviction, served by a reckless and uncompromising passion, comes not from any desire to seek conflict or defy the social order, but from a profound piety and deep domestic affection, expressed here in the unconditional love of sister for brother, "a love which death has not weakened, but only consecrated".[2]

In the opening exchange, Ismene warns her sister that she craves the impossible, that she pursues a path which can only bring death. Undaunted, Antigone spurns these words of caution, declaring that she will "suffer nothing, nothing so shameful as death without honour",[3] thereby communicating the nobility of soul which inspires her sacrifice. Her willingness to resist when there seems to be no hope, to subordinate the natural imperative of self-preservation in pursuit of something higher, however futile, is what elevates her above the commonplace and invests her death with tragic grandeur.

---

1. 991   2. Jebb, *Sophocles*   3. 120

Antigone's victory is a vindication of her devotion and the redemption, it may be said, of her troubled family, most of whom have suffered disgrace, guilty of the most egregious offences, even if unwittingly. The curse of the house of Laius leads her to an early grave, unwed and unmourned, but not in shame; for she descends to Hades "with undying glory"[1] to embrace her kin once more, loyal to her family and the laws of the gods to the very last.

---

1. 938

ἈΝΤΙΓΌΝΗ

Ἀντιγόνη

Ἀντιγόνη
ὦ κοινὸν αὐτάδελφον Ἰσμήνης κάρα,
ἆρ' οἶσθ' ὅ τι Ζεὺς τῶν ἀπ' Οἰδίπου κακῶν
ὁποῖον οὐχὶ νῷν ἔτι ζώσαιν τελεῖ;
οὐδὲν γὰρ οὔτ' ἀλγεινὸν οὔτ' ἄτης ἄτερ
οὔτ' αἰσχρὸν οὔτ' ἄτιμόν ἐσθ', ὁποῖον οὐ
τῶν σῶν τε κἀμῶν οὐκ ὄπωπ' ἐγὼ κακῶν.
καὶ νῦν τί τοῦτ' αὖ φασι πανδήμῳ πόλει
κήρυγμα θεῖναι τὸν στρατηγὸν ἀρτίως;
ἔχεις τι κεἰσήκουσας; ἤ σε λανθάνει
πρὸς τοὺς φίλους στείχοντα τῶν ἐχθρῶν κακά;   10

Ἰσμήνη
ἐμοὶ μὲν οὐδεὶς μῦθος, Ἀντιγόνη φίλων
οὔθ' ἡδὺς οὔτ' ἀλγεινὸς ἵκετ' ἐξ ὅτου
δυοῖν ἀδελφοῖν ἐστερήθημεν δύο,
μιᾷ θανόντοιν ἡμέρᾳ διπλῇ χερί·
ἐπεὶ δὲ φροῦδός ἐστιν Ἀργείων στρατὸς
ἐν νυκτὶ τῇ νῦν, οὐδὲν οἶδ' ὑπέρτερον,
οὔτ' εὐτυχοῦσα μᾶλλον οὔτ' ἀτωμένη.

Ἀντιγόνη
ᾔδη καλῶς, καί σ' ἐκτὸς αὐλείων πυλῶν
τοῦδ' οὕνεκ' ἐξέπεμπον, ὡς μόνη κλύοις.

Ἰσμήνη
τί δ' ἔστι; δηλοῖς γάρ τι καλχαίνουσ' ἔπος.   20

---
*Line numbers follow the convention established by F. Storr

Ἀντιγόνη

οὐ γὰρ τάφου νῷν τὼ κασιγνήτω Κρέων
τὸν μὲν προτίσας, τὸν δ' ἀτιμάσας ἔχει;
Ἐτεοκλέα μέν, ὡς λέγουσι, σὺν δίκης
χρήσει δικαίᾳ καὶ νόμου κατὰ χθονὸς
ἔκρυψε τοῖς ἔνερθεν ἔντιμον νεκροῖς·
τὸν δ' ἀθλίως θανόντα Πολυνείκους νέκυν
ἀστοῖσί φασιν ἐκκεκηρῦχθαι τὸ μὴ
τάφῳ καλύψαι μηδὲ κωκῦσαί τινα,
ἐᾶν δ' ἄκλαυτον, ἄταφον, οἰωνοῖς γλυκὺν
θησαυρὸν εἰσορῶσι πρὸς χάριν βορᾶς. 30
τοιαῦτά φασι τὸν ἀγαθὸν Κρέοντα σοὶ
κἀμοί, λέγω γὰρ κἀμέ, κηρύξαντ' ἔχειν,
καὶ δεῦρο νεῖσθαι ταῦτα τοῖσι μὴ εἰδόσιν
σαφῆ προκηρύξοντα, καὶ τὸ πρᾶγμ' ἄγειν
οὐχ ὡς παρ' οὐδέν, ἀλλ' ὃς ἂν τούτων τι δρᾷ,
φόνον προκεῖσθαι δημόλευστον ἐν πόλει.
οὕτως ἔχει σοι ταῦτα, καὶ δείξεις τάχα
εἴτ' εὐγενὴς πέφυκας εἴτ' ἐσθλῶν κακή.

Ἰσμήνη

τί δ', ὦ ταλαῖφρον, εἰ τάδ' ἐν τούτοις, ἐγὼ
λύουσ' ἂν ἢ 'φάπτουσα προσθείμην πλέον; 40

Ἀντιγόνη

εἰ ξυμπονήσεις καὶ ξυνεργάσει σκόπει.

Ἰσμήνη
ποῖόν τι κινδύνευμα; ποῦ γνώμης ποτ' εἶ;

Ἀντιγόνη
εἰ τὸν νεκρὸν ξὺν τῇδε κουφιεῖς χερί.

Ἰσμήνη
ἦ γὰρ νοεῖς θάπτειν σφ', ἀπόρρητον πόλει;

Ἀντιγόνη
τὸν γοῦν ἐμὸν καὶ τὸν σόν ἢν σὺ μὴ θέλῃς
ἀδελφόν: οὐ γὰρ δὴ προδοῦσ' ἁλώσομαι.

Ἰσμήνη
ὦ σχετλία, Κρέοντος ἀντειρηκότος;

Ἀντιγόνη
ἀλλ' οὐδὲν αὐτῷ τῶν ἐμῶν μ' εἴργειν μέτα.

Ἰσμήνη
οἴμοι. φρόνησον, ὦ κασιγνήτη, πατὴρ
ὡς νῷν ἀπεχθὴς δυσκλεής τ' ἀπώλετο,   50
πρὸς αὐτοφώρων ἀμπλακημάτων διπλᾶς
ὄψεις ἀράξας αὐτὸς αὐτουργῷ χερί.
ἔπειτα μήτηρ καὶ γυνή, διπλοῦν ἔπος,
πλεκταῖσιν ἀρτάναισι λωβᾶται βίον:
τρίτον δ' ἀδελφὼ δύο μίαν καθ' ἡμέραν

αὐτοκτονοῦντε τὼ ταλαιπώρω μόρον
κοινὸν κατειργάσαντ' ἐπαλλήλοιν χεροῖν.
νῦν δ' αὖ μόνα δὴ νὼ λελειμμένα σκόπει
ὅσῳ κάκιστ' ὀλούμεθ', εἰ νόμου βίᾳ
ψῆφον τυράννων ἢ κράτη παρέξιμεν. 60
ἀλλ' ἐννοεῖν χρὴ τοῦτο μὲν γυναῖχ' ὅτι
ἔφυμεν, ὡς πρὸς ἄνδρας οὐ μαχουμένα.
ἔπειτα δ' οὕνεκ' ἀρχόμεσθ' ἐκ κρεισσόνων,
καὶ ταῦτ' ἀκούειν κἄτι τῶνδ' ἀλγίονα.
ἐγὼ μὲν οὖν αἰτοῦσα τοὺς ὑπὸ χθονὸς
ξύγγνοιαν ἴσχειν, ὡς βιάζομαι τάδε,
τοῖς ἐν τέλει βεβῶσι πείσομαι: τὸ γὰρ
περισσὰ πράσσειν οὐκ ἔχει νοῦν οὐδένα.

Ἀντιγόνη
οὔτ' ἂν κελεύσαιμ' οὔτ' ἄν, εἰ θέλοις ἔτι
πράσσειν, ἐμοῦ γ' ἂν ἡδέως δρῴης μέτα. 70
ἀλλ' ἴσθ' ὁποῖά σοι δοκεῖ, κεῖνον δ' ἐγὼ
θάψω: καλόν μοι τοῦτο ποιούσῃ θανεῖν.
φίλη μετ' αὐτοῦ κείσομαι, φίλου μέτα,
ὅσια πανουργήσασ'. ἐπεὶ πλείων χρόνος
ὃν δεῖ μ' ἀρέσκειν τοῖς κάτω τῶν ἐνθάδε.
ἐκεῖ γὰρ αἰεὶ κείσομαι: σοὶ δ', εἰ δοκεῖ,
τὰ τῶν θεῶν ἔντιμ' ἀτιμάσασ' ἔχε.

Ἰσμήνη
ἐγὼ μὲν οὐκ ἄτιμα ποιοῦμαι, τὸ δὲ
βίᾳ πολιτῶν δρᾶν ἔφυν ἀμήχανος.

Ἀντιγόνη
σὺ μὲν τάδ᾽ ἂν προὔχοι᾽· ἐγὼ δὲ δὴ τάφον   80
χώσουσ᾽ ἀδελφῷ φιλτάτῳ πορεύσομαι.

Ἰσμήνη
οἴμοι ταλαίνης, ὡς ὑπερδέδοικά σου.

Ἀντιγόνη
μὴ 'μοῦ προτάρβει· τὸν σὸν ἐξόρθου πότμον.

Ἰσμήνη
ἀλλ᾽ οὖν προμηνύσῃς γε τοῦτο μηδενὶ
τοὔργον, κρυφῇ δὲ κεῦθε, σὺν δ᾽ αὔτως ἐγώ.

Ἀντιγόνη
οἴμοι, καταύδα· πολλὸν ἐχθίων ἔσει
σιγῶσ᾽, ἐὰν μὴ πᾶσι κηρύξῃς τάδε.

Ἰσμήνη
θερμὴν ἐπὶ ψυχροῖσι καρδίαν ἔχεις.

Ἀντιγόνη
ἀλλ᾽ οἶδ᾽ ἀρέσκουσ᾽ οἷς μάλισθ᾽ ἁδεῖν με χρή.

Ἰσμήνη
εἰ καὶ δυνήσει γ᾽· ἀλλ᾽ ἀμηχάνων ἐρᾷς.   90

Ἀντιγόνη
οὔκουν, ὅταν δὴ μὴ σθένω, πεπαύσομαι.

Ἰσμήνη
ἀρχὴν δὲ θηρᾶν οὐ πρέπει τἀμήχανα.

Ἀντιγόνη
εἰ ταῦτα λέξεις, ἐχθαρεῖ μὲν ἐξ ἐμοῦ,
ἐχθρὰ δὲ τῷ θανόντι προσκείσει δίκῃ.
ἀλλ' ἔα με καὶ τὴν ἐξ ἐμοῦ δυσβουλίαν
παθεῖν τὸ δεινὸν τοῦτο: πείσομαι γὰρ οὐ
τοσοῦτον οὐδὲν ὥστε μὴ οὐ καλῶς θανεῖν.

Ἰσμήνη
ἀλλ' εἰ δοκεῖ σοι, στεῖχε: τοῦτο δ' ἴσθ' ὅτι
ἄνους μὲν ἔρχει, τοῖς φίλοις δ' ὀρθῶς φίλη.

Χορός
ἀκτὶς ἀελίου, τὸ κάλλιστον ἑπταπύλῳ φανὲν   100
Θήβᾳ τῶν προτέρων φάος,
ἐφάνθης ποτ', ὦ χρυσέας
ἁμέρας βλέφαρον,
Διρκαίων ὑπὲρ ῥεέθρων μολοῦσα,
τὸν λεύκασπιν Ἀργόθεν ἐκβάντα φῶτα πανσαγίᾳ
φυγάδα πρόδρομον ὀξυτέρῳ κινήσασα χαλινῷ:
ὃς ἐφ' ἡμετέρᾳ γᾷ Πολυνείκους   110
ἀρθεὶς νεικέων ἐξ ἀμφιλόγων
ὀξέα κλάζων

ἀετὸς εἰς γᾶν ὣς ὑπερέπτα,
λευκῆς χιόνος πτέρυγι στεγανός,
πολλῶν μεθ' ὅπλων
ξύν θ' ἱπποκόμοις κορύθεσσιν.

στὰς δ' ὑπὲρ μελάθρων φονώσαισιν ἀμφιχανὼν κύκλῳ
λόγχαις ἑπτάπυλον στόμα
ἔβα, πρίν ποθ' ἁμετέρων
αἱμάτων γένυσιν πλησθῆναί τε καὶ στεφάνωμα πύργων   120
πευκάενθ' Ἥφαιστον ἑλεῖν. τοῖος ἀμφὶ νῶτ' ἐτάθη
πάταγος Ἄρεος, ἀντιπάλῳ δυσχείρωμα δράκοντος.

Ζεὺς γὰρ μεγάλης γλώσσης κόμπους
ὑπερεχθαίρει, καὶ σφας ἐσιδὼν
πολλῷ ῥεύματι προσνισσομένους
χρυσοῦ καναχῆς ὑπεροπλίαις,   130
παλτῷ ῥιπτεῖ πυρὶ βαλβίδων
ἐπ' ἄκρων ἤδη
νίκην ὁρμῶντ' ἀλαλάξαι.

ἀντιτύπᾳ δ' ἐπὶ γᾷ πέσε τανταλωθεὶς
πυρφόρος, ὃς τότε μαινομένᾳ ξὺν ὁρμᾷ
βακχεύων ἐπέπνει
ῥιπαῖς ἐχθίστων ἀνέμων.
εἶχε δ' ἄλλα τὰ μέν,
ἄλλα δ' ἐπ' ἄλλοις ἐπενώμα στυφελίζων
μέγας Ἄρης δεξιόσειρος.   140

ἑπτὰ λοχαγοὶ γὰρ ἐφ' ἑπτὰ πύλαις
ταχθέντες ἴσοι πρὸς ἴσους ἔλιπον
Ζηνὶ τροπαίῳ πάγχαλκα τέλη,
πλὴν τοῖν στυγεροῖν, ὣ πατρὸς ἑνὸς
μητρός τε μιᾶς φύντε καθ' αὑτοῖν
δικρατεῖς λόγχας στήσαντ' ἔχετον
κοινοῦ θανάτου μέρος ἄμφω.

ἀλλὰ γὰρ ἁ μεγαλώνυμος ἦλθε Νίκα
τᾷ πολυαρμάτῳ ἀντιχαρεῖσα Θήβᾳ,
ἐκ μὲν δὴ πολέμων   150
τῶν νῦν θέσθαι λησμοσύναν,
θεῶν δὲ ναοὺς χοροῖς
παννυχίοις πάντας ἐπέλθωμεν,
ὁ Θήβας δ' ἐλελίχθων Βάκχιος ἄρχοι.

ἀλλ' ὅδε γὰρ δὴ βασιλεὺς χώρας,
Κρέων ὁ Μενοικέως ἄρχων νεοχμὸς
νεαραῖσι θεῶν ἐπὶ συντυχίαις
χωρεῖ, τίνα δὴ μῆτιν ἐρέσσων,
ὅτι σύγκλητον τήνδε γερόντων   160
προὔθετο λέσχην,
κοινῷ κηρύγματι πέμψας;

Κρέων
ἄνδρες, τὰ μὲν δὴ πόλεος ἀσφαλῶς θεοὶ
πολλῷ σάλῳ σείσαντες ὤρθωσαν πάλιν.
ὑμᾶς δ' ἐγὼ πομποῖσιν ἐκ πάντων δίχα

ἔστειλ᾽ ἱκέσθαι τοῦτο μὲν τὰ Λαΐου
σέβοντας εἰδὼς εὖ θρόνων ἀεὶ κράτη,
τοῦτ᾽ αὖθις, ἡνίκ᾽ Οἰδίπους ὤρθου πόλιν,
κἀπεὶ διώλετ᾽, ἀμφὶ τοὺς κείνων ἔτι
παῖδας μένοντας ἐμπέδοις φρονήμασιν.
ὅτ᾽ οὖν ἐκεῖνοι πρὸς διπλῆς μοίρας μίαν 170
καθ᾽ ἡμέραν ὤλοντο παίσαντές τε καὶ
πληγέντες αὐτόχειρι σὺν μιάσματι,
ἐγὼ κράτη δὴ πάντα καὶ θρόνους ἔχω
γένους κατ᾽ ἀγχιστεῖα τῶν ὀλωλότων.
ἀμήχανον δὲ παντὸς ἀνδρὸς ἐκμαθεῖν
ψυχήν τε καὶ φρόνημα καὶ γνώμην, πρὶν ἂν
ἀρχαῖς τε καὶ νόμοισιν ἐντριβὴς φανῇ.
ἐμοὶ γὰρ ὅστις πᾶσαν εὐθύνων πόλιν
μὴ τῶν ἀρίστων ἅπτεται βουλευμάτων
ἀλλ᾽ ἐκ φόβου του γλῶσσαν ἐγκλῄσας ἔχει 180
κάκιστος εἶναι νῦν τε καὶ πάλαι δοκεῖ·
καὶ μεῖζον ὅστις ἀντὶ τῆς αὑτοῦ πάτρας
φίλον νομίζει, τοῦτον οὐδαμοῦ λέγω.
ἐγὼ γάρ, ἴστω Ζεὺς ὁ πάνθ᾽ ὁρῶν ἀεί,
οὔτ᾽ ἂν σιωπήσαιμι τὴν ἄτην ὁρῶν
στείχουσαν ἀστοῖς ἀντὶ τῆς σωτηρίας,
οὔτ᾽ ἂν φίλον ποτ᾽ ἄνδρα δυσμενῆ χθονὸς
θείμην ἐμαυτῷ, τοῦτο γιγνώσκων ὅτι
ἥδ᾽ ἐστὶν ἡ σῴζουσα καὶ ταύτης ἔπι
πλέοντες ὀρθῆς τοὺς φίλους ποιούμεθα. 190
τοιοῖσδ᾽ ἐγὼ νόμοισι τήνδ᾽ αὔξω πόλιν,
καὶ νῦν ἀδελφὰ τῶνδε κηρύξας ἔχω

ἀστοῖσι παίδων τῶν ἀπ' Οἰδίπου πέρι·
Ἐτεοκλέα μέν, ὃς πόλεως ὑπερμαχῶν
ὄλωλε τῆσδε, πάντ' ἀριστεύσας δόρει,
τάφῳ τε κρύψαι καὶ τὰ πάντ' ἀφαγνίσαι
ἃ τοῖς ἀρίστοις ἔρχεται κάτω νεκροῖς.
τὸν δ' αὖ ξύναιμον τοῦδε, Πολυνείκη λέγω,
ὃς γῆν πατρῴαν καὶ θεοὺς τοὺς ἐγγενεῖς
φυγὰς κατελθὼν ἠθέλησε μὲν πυρὶ   200
πρῆσαι κατ' ἄκρας, ἠθέλησε δ' αἵματος
κοινοῦ πάσασθαι, τοὺς δὲ δουλώσας ἄγειν,
τοῦτον πόλει τῇδ' ἐκκεκήρυκται τάφῳ
μήτε κτερίζειν μήτε κωκῦσαί τινα,
ἐᾶν δ' ἄθαπτον καὶ πρὸς οἰωνῶν δέμας
καὶ πρὸς κυνῶν ἐδεστὸν αἰκισθέν τ' ἰδεῖν.
τοιόνδ' ἐμὸν φρόνημα, κοὔποτ' ἔκ γ' ἐμοῦ
τιμὴν προέξουσ' οἱ κακοὶ τῶν ἐνδίκων·
ἀλλ' ὅστις εὔνους τῇδε τῇ πόλει, θανὼν
καὶ ζῶν ὁμοίως ἐξ ἐμοῦ τιμήσεται.   210

Χορός
σοὶ ταῦτ' ἀρέσκει, παῖ Μενοικέως Κρέον,
τὸν τῇδε δύσνουν κὰς τὸν εὐμενῆ πόλει·
νόμῳ δὲ χρῆσθαι παντί που πάρεστί σοι
καὶ τῶν θανόντων χὠπόσοι ζῶμεν πέρι.

Κρέων
ὡς ἂν σκοποὶ νῦν εἶτε τῶν εἰρημένων.

Χορός
νεωτέρῳ τῳ τοῦτο βαστάζειν πρόθες.

Κρέων
ἀλλ' εἴσ' ἑτοῖμοι τοῦ νεκροῦ γ' ἐπίσκοποι.

Χορός
τί δῆτ' ἂν ἄλλο τοῦτ' ἐπεντέλλοις ἔτι;

Κρέων
τὸ μὴ 'πιχωρεῖν τοῖς ἀπιστοῦσιν τάδε.

Χορός
οὐκ ἔστιν οὕτω μῶρος ὃς θανεῖν ἐρᾷ.   220

Κρέων
καὶ μὴν ὁ μισθός γ', οὗτος: ἀλλ' ὑπ' ἐλπίδων
ἄνδρας τὸ κέρδος πολλάκις διώλεσεν.

Φύλαξ
ἄναξ, ἐρῶ μὲν οὐχ ὅπως τάχους ὕπο
δύσπνους ἱκάνω κοῦφον ἐξάρας πόδα.
πολλὰς γὰρ ἔσχον φροντίδων ἐπιστάσεις,
ὁδοῖς κυκλῶν ἐμαυτὸν εἰς ἀναστροφήν:
ψυχὴ γὰρ ηὔδα πολλά μοι μυθουμένη:
τάλας, τί χωρεῖς οἷ μολὼν δώσεις δίκην;
τλήμων, μενεῖς αὖ; κεἰ τάδ' εἴσεται Κρέων

ἄλλου παρ' ἀνδρός; πῶς σὺ δῆτ' οὐκ ἀλγύνει; 230
τοιαῦθ' ἑλίσσων ἤνυτον σχολῇ βραδύς.
χοὔτως ὁδὸς βραχεῖα γίγνεται μακρά.
τέλος γε μέντοι δεῦρ' ἐνίκησεν μολεῖν
σοί. κεἰ τὸ μηδὲν ἐξερῶ, φράσω δ' ὅμως·
τῆς ἐλπίδος γὰρ ἔρχομαι δεδραγμένος,
τὸ μὴ παθεῖν ἂν ἄλλο πλὴν τὸ μόρσιμον.

Κρέων
τί δ' ἐστὶν ἀνθ' οὗ τήνδ' ἔχεις ἀθυμίαν;

Φύλαξ
φράσαι θέλω σοι πρῶτα τἀμαυτοῦ· τὸ γὰρ
πρᾶγμ' οὔτ' ἔδρασ' οὔτ' εἶδον ὅστις ἦν ὁ δρῶν,
οὐδ' ἂν δικαίως ἐς κακὸν πέσοιμί τι. 240

Κρέων
εὖ γε στοχάζει κἀποφάργνυσαι κύκλῳ
τὸ πρᾶγμα· δηλοῖς δ' ὥς τι σημανῶν νέον.

Φύλαξ
τὰ δεινὰ γάρ τοι προστίθησ' ὄκνον πολύν.

Κρέων
οὔκουν ἐρεῖς ποτ', εἶτ' ἀπαλλαχθεὶς ἄπει;

Φύλαξ
καὶ δὴ λέγω σοι. τὸν νεκρόν τις ἀρτίως
θάψας βέβηκε κἀπὶ χρωτὶ διψίαν
κόνιν παλύνας κἀφαγιστεύσας ἃ χρή·

Κρέων
τί φής; τίς ἀνδρῶν ἦν ὁ τολμήσας τάδε;

Φύλαξ
οὐκ οἶδ'· ἐκεῖ γὰρ οὔτε του γενῇδος ἦν
πλῆγμ', οὐ δικέλλης ἐκβολή. στύφλος δὲ γῆ 250
καὶ χέρσος, ἀρρὼξ οὐδ' ἐπημαξευμένη
τροχοῖσιν, ἀλλ' ἄσημος οὑργάτης τις ἦν.
ὅπως δ' ὁ πρῶτος ἡμὶν ἡμεροσκόπος
δείκνυσι, πᾶσι θαῦμα δυσχερὲς παρῆν.
ὁ μὲν γὰρ ἠφάνιστο, τυμβήρης μὲν οὔ,
λεπτὴ δ', ἄγος φεύγοντος ὥς, ἐπῆν κόνις·
σημεῖα δ' οὔτε θηρὸς οὔτε του κυνῶν
ἐλθόντος, οὐ σπάσαντος ἐξεφαίνετο.
λόγοι δ' ἐν ἀλλήλοισιν ἐρρόθουν κακοί,
φύλαξ ἐλέγχων φύλακα, κἂν ἐγίγνετο 260
πληγὴ τελευτῶσ', οὐδ' ὁ κωλύσων παρῆν.
εἷς γάρ τις ἦν ἕκαστος οὑξειργασμένος,
κοὐδεὶς ἐναργής, ἀλλ' ἔφευγε μὴ εἰδέναι.
ἦμεν δ' ἕτοιμοι καὶ μύδρους αἴρειν χεροῖν
καὶ πῦρ διέρπειν καὶ θεοὺς ὀρκωμοτεῖν,
τὸ μήτε δρᾶσαι μήτε τῳ ξυνειδέναι
τὸ πρᾶγμα βουλεύσαντι μηδ' εἰργασμένῳ.

τέλος δ' ὅτ' οὐδὲν ἦν ἐρευνῶσιν πλέον,
λέγει τις εἷς, ὃ πάντας ἐς πέδον κάρα
νεῦσαι φόβῳ προύτρεψεν· οὐ γὰρ εἴχομεν 270
οὔτ' ἀντιφωνεῖν οὔθ' ὅπως δρῶντες καλῶς
πράξαιμεν. ἦν δ' ὁ μῦθος ὡς ἀνοιστέον
σοὶ τοὔργον εἴη τοῦτο κοὐχὶ κρυπτέον.
καὶ ταῦτ' ἐνίκα, κἀμὲ τὸν δυσδαίμονα
πάλος καθαιρεῖ τοῦτο τἀγαθὸν λαβεῖν.
πάρειμι δ' ἄκων οὐχ ἑκοῦσιν, οἶδ' ὅτι·
στέργει γὰρ οὐδεὶς ἄγγελον κακῶν ἐπῶν.

Χορός
ἄναξ, ἐμοί τοι, μή τι καὶ θεήλατον
τοὔργον τόδ', ἡ ξύννοια βουλεύει πάλαι

Κρέων
παῦσαι, πρὶν ὀργῆς καὶ 'μὲ μεστῶσαι λέγων, 280
μὴ 'φευρεθῇς ἄνους τε καὶ γέρων ἅμα.
λέγεις γὰρ οὐκ ἀνεκτὰ δαίμονας λέγων
πρόνοιαν ἴσχειν τοῦδε τοῦ νεκροῦ πέρι.
πότερον ὑπερτιμῶντες ὡς εὐεργέτην
ἔκρυπτον αὐτόν, ὅστις ἀμφικίονας
ναοὺς πυρώσων ἦλθε κἀναθήματα
καὶ γῆν ἐκείνων καὶ νόμους διασκεδῶν;
ἢ τοὺς κακοὺς τιμῶντας εἰσορᾷς θεούς;
οὐκ ἔστιν. ἀλλὰ ταῦτα καὶ πάλαι πόλεως
ἄνδρες μόλις φέροντες ἐρρόθουν ἐμοί, 290
κρυφῇ κάρα σείοντες, οὐδ' ὑπὸ ζυγῷ

λόφον δικαίως εἶχον, ὡς στέργειν ἐμέ.
ἐκ τῶνδε τούτους ἐξεπίσταμαι καλῶς
παρηγμένους μισθοῖσιν εἰργάσθαι τάδε.
οὐδὲν γὰρ ἀνθρώποισιν οἷον ἄργυρος
κακὸν νόμισμ᾽ ἔβλαστε. τοῦτο καὶ πόλεις
πορθεῖ, τόδ᾽ ἄνδρας ἐξανίστησιν δόμων·
τόδ᾽ ἐκδιδάσκει καὶ παραλλάσσει φρένας
χρηστὰς πρὸς αἰσχρὰ πράγματ᾽ ἵστασθαι βροτῶν·
πανουργίας δ᾽ ἔδειξεν ἀνθρώποις ἔχειν 300
καὶ παντὸς ἔργου δυσσέβειαν εἰδέναι.
ὅσοι δὲ μισθαρνοῦντες ἤνυσαν τάδε,
χρόνῳ ποτ᾽ ἐξέπραξαν ὡς δοῦναι δίκην.
ἀλλ᾽ εἴπερ ἴσχει Ζεὺς ἔτ᾽ ἐξ ἐμοῦ σέβας,
εὖ τοῦτ᾽ ἐπίστασ᾽, ὅρκιος δέ σοι λέγω·
εἰ μὴ τὸν αὐτόχειρα τοῦδε τοῦ τάφου
εὑρόντες ἐκφανεῖτ᾽ ἐς ὀφθαλμοὺς ἐμούς,
οὐχ ὑμὶν Ἅιδης μοῦνος ἀρκέσει, πρὶν ἂν
ζῶντες κρεμαστοὶ τήνδε δηλώσηθ᾽ ὕβριν,
ἵν᾽ εἰδότες τὸ κέρδος ἔνθεν οἰστέον 310
τὸ λοιπὸν ἁρπάζητε, καὶ μάθηθ᾽ ὅτι
οὐκ ἐξ ἅπαντος δεῖ τὸ κερδαίνειν φιλεῖν.
ἐκ τῶν γὰρ αἰσχρῶν λημμάτων τοὺς πλείονας
ἀτωμένους ἴδοις ἂν ἢ σεσωσμένους.

Φύλαξ
εἰπεῖν τι δώσεις ἢ στραφεὶς οὕτως ἴω;

ANTIGONE

Κρέων
οὐκ οἶσθα καὶ νῦν ὡς ἀνιαρῶς λέγεις;

Φύλαξ
ἐν τοῖσιν ὠσὶν ἢ 'πὶ τῇ ψυχῇ δάκνει;

Κρέων
τί δὲ ῥυθμίζεις τὴν ἐμὴν λύπην ὅπου;

Φύλαξ
ὁ δρῶν σ' ἀνιᾷ τὰς φρένας, τὰ δ' ὦτ' ἐγώ.

Κρέων
οἴμ' ὡς λάλημα δῆλον ἐκπεφυκὸς εἶ. 320

Φύλαξ
οὔκουν τό γ' ἔργον τοῦτο ποιήσας ποτέ.

Κρέων
καὶ ταῦτ' ἐπ' ἀργύρῳ γε τὴν ψυχὴν προδούς.

Φύλαξ
Φεῦ: ἦ δεινὸν ᾧ δοκῇ γε καὶ ψευδῆ δοκεῖν.

Κρέων
κόμψευέ νυν τὴν δόξαν: εἰ δὲ ταῦτα μὴ
φανεῖτέ μοι τοὺς δρῶντας, ἐξερεῖθ' ὅτι

τὰ δειλὰ κέρδη πημονὰς ἐργάζεται.

Φύλαξ
ἀλλ' εὑρεθείη μὲν μάλιστ'· ἐὰν δέ τοι
ληφθῇ τε καὶ μή, τοῦτο γὰρ τύχη κρινεῖ,
οὐκ ἔσθ' ὅπως ὄψει σὺ δεῦρ' ἐλθόντα με·
καὶ νῦν γὰρ ἐκτὸς ἐλπίδος γνώμης τ' ἐμῆς   330
σωθεὶς ὀφείλω τοῖς θεοῖς πολλὴν χάριν.

Χορός
πολλὰ τὰ δεινὰ κοὐδὲν
ἀνθρώπου δεινότερον πέλει.
τοῦτο καὶ πολιοῦ πέραν πόντου
χειμερίῳ νότῳ χωρεῖ,
Περιβρυχίοισιν περῶν ὑπ' οἴδμασιν.
θεῶν τε τὰν ὑπερτάταν, Γᾶν
ἄφθιτον, ἀκαμάταν, ἀποτρύεται
ἰλλομένων ἀρότρων ἔτος εἰς ἔτος
ἱππείῳ γένει πολεύων.   340

κουφονόων τε φῦλον ὀρνίθων
ἀμφιβαλὼν ἄγει
καὶ θηρῶν ἀγρίων ἔθνη
πόντου τ' εἰναλίαν φύσιν
σπείραισι δικτυοκλώστοις,
περιφραδὴς ἀνήρ·
κρατεῖ δὲ μηχαναῖς ἀγραύλου
θηρὸς ὀρεσσιβάτα, λασιαύχενά θ'   350

ἵππον ὀχμάζεται ἀμφὶ λόφον ζυγῶν
οὔρειόν τ' ἀκμῆτα ταῦρον.

καὶ φθέγμα καὶ ἀνεμόεν φρόνημα καὶ ἀστυνόμους
ὀργὰς ἐδιδάξατο καὶ δυσαύλων
πάγων ὑπαίθρεια καὶ δύσομβρα φεύγειν βέλη
παντοπόρος· ἄπορος ἐπ' οὐδὲν ἔρχεται
τὸ μέλλον· Ἅιδα μόνον φεῦξιν οὐκ ἐπάξεται· 360
νόσων δ' ἀμηχάνων φυγὰς ξυμπέφρασται.

σοφόν τι τὸ μηχανόεν τέχνας ὑπὲρ ἐλπίδ' ἔχων
τοτὲ μὲν κακόν, ἄλλοτ' ἐπ' ἐσθλὸν ἕρπει,
νόμους γεραίρων χθονὸς θεῶν τ' ἔνορκον δίκαν,
ὑψίπολις· ἄπολις ὅτῳ τὸ μὴ καλὸν 370
ξύνεστι τόλμας χάριν. μήτ' ἐμοὶ παρέστιος
γένοιτο μήτ' ἴσον φρονῶν ὃς τάδ' ἔρδει.

ἐς δαιμόνιον τέρας ἀμφινοῶ
τόδε· πῶς εἰδὼς ἀντιλογήσω
τήνδ' οὐκ εἶναι παῖδ' Ἀντιγόνην.
ὦ δύστηνος
καὶ δυστήνου πατρὸς Οἰδιπόδα, 380
τί ποτ'; οὐ δή που σέ γ' ἀπιστοῦσαν
τοῖς βασιλείοισιν ἄγουσι νόμοις
καὶ ἐν ἀφροσύνῃ καθελόντες;

Φύλαξ
ἥδ' ἔστ' ἐκείνη τοὔργον ἡ 'ξειργασμένη·

τήνδ' εἵλομεν θάπτουσαν. ἀλλὰ ποῦ Κρέων;

Χορός
ὅδ' ἐκ δόμων ἄψορρος εἰς δέον περᾷ.

Κρέων
τί δ' ἔστι; ποίᾳ ξύμμετρος προὔβην τύχῃ;

Φύλαξ
ἄναξ, βροτοῖσιν οὐδέν ἔστ' ἀπώμοτον.
ψεύδει γὰρ ἡ 'πίνοια τὴν γνώμην· ἐπεὶ
σχολῇ ποθ' ἥξειν δεῦρ' ἂν ἐξηύχουν ἐγὼ   390
ταῖς σαῖς ἀπειλαῖς αἷς ἐχειμάσθην τότε·
ἀλλ' ἡ γὰρ ἐκτὸς καὶ παρ' ἐλπίδας χαρὰ
ἔοικεν ἄλλῃ μῆκος οὐδὲν ἡδονῇ,
ἥκω, δι' ὅρκων καίπερ ὢν ἀπώμοτος,
κόρην ἄγων τήνδ', ἣ καθῃρέθη τάφον
κοσμοῦσα. κλῆρος ἐνθάδ' οὐκ ἐπάλλετο,
ἀλλ' ἔστ' ἐμὸν θοὔρμαιον, οὐκ ἄλλου, τόδε.
καὶ νῦν, ἄναξ, τήνδ' αὐτός, ὡς θέλεις, λαβὼν
καὶ κρῖνε κἀξέλεγχ'· ἐγὼ δ' ἐλεύθερος
δίκαιός εἰμι τῶνδ' ἀπηλλάχθαι κακῶν.   400

Κρέων
ἄγεις δὲ τήνδε τῷ τρόπῳ πόθεν λαβών;

Φύλαξ
αὕτη τὸν ἄνδρ' ἔθαπτε· πάντ' ἐπίστασαι.

Κρέων
ἦ καὶ ξυνίης καὶ λέγεις ὀρθῶς ἃ φῄς;

Φύλαξ
ταύτην γ' ἰδὼν θάπτουσαν ὃν σὺ τὸν νεκρὸν
ἀπεῖπας. ἆρ' ἔνδηλα καὶ σαφῆ λέγω;

Κρέων
καὶ πῶς ὁρᾶται κἀπίληπτος ᾑρέθη;

Φύλαξ
τοιοῦτον ἦν τὸ πρᾶγμ'. ὅπως γὰρ ἥκομεν,
πρὸς σοῦ τὰ δείν' ἐκεῖν' ἐπηπειλημένοι,
πᾶσαν κόνιν σήραντες, ἣ κατεῖχε τὸν
νέκυν, μυδῶν τε σῶμα γυμνώσαντες εὖ, 410
καθήμεθ' ἄκρων ἐκ πάγων ὑπήνεμοι,
ὀσμὴν ἀπ' αὐτοῦ μὴ βάλοι πεφευγότες,
ἐγερτὶ κινῶν ἄνδρ' ἀνὴρ ἐπιρρόθοις
κακοῖσιν, εἴ τις τοῦδ' ἀκηδήσοι πόνου.
χρόνον τάδ' ἦν τοσοῦτον, ἔστ' ἐν αἰθέρι
μέσῳ κατέστη λαμπρὸς ἡλίου κύκλος
καὶ καῦμ' ἔθαλπε: καὶ τότ' ἐξαίφνης χθονὸς
τυφὼς ἀείρας σκηπτόν οὐράνιον ἄχος,
πίμπλησι πεδίον, πᾶσαν αἰκίζων φόβην
ὕλης πεδιάδος, ἐν δ' ἐμεστώθη μέγας 420
αἰθήρ: μύσαντες δ' εἴχομεν θείαν νόσον.
καὶ τοῦδ' ἀπαλλαγέντος ἐν χρόνῳ μακρῷ,
ἡ παῖς ὁρᾶται, κἀνακωκύει πικρᾶς

ὄρνιθος ὀξὺν φθόγγον, ἐς ὅταν κενῆς
εὐνῆς νεοσσῶν ὀρφανὸν βλέψῃ λέχος.
οὕτω δὲ χαὔτη, ψιλὸν ὡς ὁρᾷ νέκυν,
γόοισιν ἐξώμωξεν, ἐκ δ' ἀρὰς κακὰς
ἠρᾶτο τοῖσι τοὔργον ἐξειργασμένοις.
καὶ χερσὶν εὐθὺς διψίαν φέρει κόνιν,
ἔκ τ' εὐκροτήτου χαλκέας ἄρδην πρόχου 430
χοαῖσι τρισπόνδοισι τὸν νέκυν στέφει.
χἠμεῖς ἰδόντες ἱέμεσθα, σὺν δέ νιν
θηρώμεθ' εὐθὺς οὐδὲν ἐκπεπληγμένην,
καὶ τάς τε πρόσθεν τάς τε νῦν ἠλέγχομεν
πράξεις: ἄπαρνος δ' οὐδενὸς καθίστατο,
ἅμ' ἡδέως ἔμοιγε κἀλγεινῶς ἅμα.
τὸ μὲν γὰρ αὐτὸν ἐκ κακῶν πεφευγέναι
ἥδιστον, ἐς κακὸν δὲ τοὺς φίλους ἄγειν
ἀλγεινόν: ἀλλὰ πάντα ταῦθ' ἥσσω λαβεῖν
ἐμοὶ πέφυκε τῆς ἐμῆς σωτηρίας. 440

Κρέων
σὲ δή, σὲ τὴν νεύουσαν εἰς πέδον κάρα,
φῂς ἢ καταρνεῖ μὴ δεδρακέναι τάδε:

Ἀντιγόνη
καὶ φημὶ δρᾶσαι κοὐκ ἀπαρνοῦμαι τὸ μή.

Κρέων
σὺ μὲν κομίζοις ἂν σεαυτὸν ᾗ θέλεις
ἔξω βαρείας αἰτίας ἐλεύθερον:

σὺ δ' εἰπέ μοι μὴ μῆκος, ἀλλὰ συντόμως,
ᾔδησθα κηρυχθέντα μὴ πράσσειν τάδε;

Ἀντιγόνη
ᾔδη: τί δ' οὐκ ἔμελλον; ἐμφανῆ γὰρ ἦν.

Κρέων
καὶ δῆτ' ἐτόλμας τούσδ' ὑπερβαίνειν νόμους;

Ἀντιγόνη
οὐ γάρ τί μοι Ζεὺς ἦν ὁ κηρύξας τάδε, 450
οὐδ' ἡ ξύνοικος τῶν κάτω θεῶν Δίκη
τοιούσδ' ἐν ἀνθρώποισιν ὥρισεν νόμους.
οὐδὲ σθένειν τοσοῦτον ᾠόμην τὰ σὰ
κηρύγμαθ', ὥστ' ἄγραπτα κἀσφαλῆ θεῶν
νόμιμα δύνασθαι θνητὸν ὄνθ' ὑπερδραμεῖν.
οὐ γάρ τι νῦν γε κἀχθές, ἀλλ' ἀεί ποτε
ζῇ ταῦτα, κοὐδεὶς οἶδεν ἐξ ὅτου 'φάνη.
τούτων ἐγὼ οὐκ ἔμελλον, ἀνδρὸς οὐδενὸς
φρόνημα δείσασ', ἐν θεοῖσι τὴν δίκην
δώσειν: θανουμένη γὰρ ἐξῄδη, τί δ' οὔ; 460
κεἰ μὴ σὺ προὐκήρυξας. εἰ δὲ τοῦ χρόνου
πρόσθεν θανοῦμαι, κέρδος αὔτ' ἐγὼ λέγω.
ὅστις γὰρ ἐν πολλοῖσιν ὡς ἐγὼ κακοῖς
ζῇ, πῶς ὅδ' Οὐχὶ κατθανὼν κέρδος φέρει;
οὕτως ἔμοιγε τοῦδε τοῦ μόρου τυχεῖν
παρ' οὐδὲν ἄλγος: ἀλλ' ἄν, εἰ τὸν ἐξ ἐμῆς
μητρὸς θανόντ' ἄθαπτον ἠνσχόμην νέκυν,

κείνοις ἂν ἤλγουν· τοῖσδε δ' οὐκ ἀλγύνομαι.
σοὶ δ' εἰ δοκῶ νῦν μῶρα δρῶσα τυγχάνειν,
σχεδόν τι μώρῳ μωρίαν ὀφλισκάνω. 470

Χορός
δηλοῖ τὸ γέννημ' ὠμὸν ἐξ ὠμοῦ πατρὸς
τῆς παιδός. εἴκειν δ' οὐκ ἐπίσταται κακοῖς.

Κρέων
ἀλλ' ἴσθι τοι τὰ σκλήρ' ἄγαν φρονήματα
πίπτειν μάλιστα, καὶ τὸν ἐγκρατέστατον
σίδηρον ὀπτὸν ἐκ πυρὸς περισκελῆ
θραυσθέντα καὶ ῥαγέντα πλεῖστ' ἂν εἰσίδοις·
σμικρῷ χαλινῷ δ' οἶδα τοὺς θυμουμένους
ἵππους καταρτυθέντας· οὐ γὰρ ἐκπέλει
φρονεῖν μέγ' ὅστις δοῦλός ἐστι τῶν πέλας.
αὕτη δ' ὑβρίζειν μὲν τότ' ἐξηπίστατο, 480
νόμους ὑπερβαίνουσα τοὺς προκειμένους·
ὕβρις δ', ἐπεὶ δέδρακεν, ἥδε δευτέρα,
τούτοις ἐπαυχεῖν καὶ δεδρακυῖαν γελᾶν.
ἦ νῦν ἐγὼ μὲν οὐκ ἀνήρ, αὕτη δ' ἀνήρ,
εἰ ταῦτ' ἀνατὶ τῇδε κείσεται κράτη.
ἀλλ' εἴτ' ἀδελφῆς εἴθ' ὁμαιμονεστέρα
τοῦ παντὸς ἡμῖν Ζηνὸς ἑρκείου κυρεῖ,
αὐτή τε χἠ ξύναιμος οὐκ ἀλύξετον
μόρου κακίστου· καὶ γὰρ οὖν κείνην ἴσον
ἐπαιτιῶμαι τοῦδε βουλεῦσαι τάφου. 490
καί νιν καλεῖτ'· ἔσω γὰρ εἶδον ἀρτίως

λυσσῶσαν αὐτὴν οὐδ' ἐπήβολον φρενῶν.
φιλεῖ δ' ὁ θυμὸς πρόσθεν, ἠρῆσθαι κλοπεὺς
τῶν μηδὲν ὀρθῶς ἐν σκότῳ τεχνωμένων·
μισῶ γε μέντοι χὤταν ἐν κακοῖσί τις
ἁλοὺς ἔπειτα τοῦτο καλλύνειν θέλῃ.

Ἀντιγόνη
θέλεις τι μεῖζον ἢ κατακτεῖναί μ' ἑλών;

Κρέων
ἐγὼ μὲν οὐδέν· τοῦτ' ἔχων ἅπαντ' ἔχω.

Ἀντιγόνη
τί δῆτα μέλλεις; ὡς ἐμοὶ τῶν σῶν λόγων
ἀρεστὸν οὐδὲν μηδ' ἀρεσθείη ποτέ· 500
οὕτω δὲ καὶ σοὶ τἄμ' ἀφανδάνοντ' ἔφυ.
καίτοι πόθεν κλέος γ' ἂν εὐκλεέστερον
κατέσχον ἢ τὸν αὐτάδελφον ἐν τάφῳ
τιθεῖσα; τούτοις τοῦτο πᾶσιν ἁνδάνειν
λέγοιτ' ἄν, εἰ μὴ γλῶσσαν ἐγκλῄοι φόβος.
ἀλλ' ἡ τυραννὶς πολλά τ' ἄλλ' εὐδαιμονεῖ
κἄξεστιν αὐτῇ δρᾶν λέγειν θ' ἃ βούλεται.

Κρέων
σὺ τοῦτο μούνη τῶνδε Καδμείων ὁρᾷς.

Ἀντιγόνη
ὁρῶσι χοὗτοι, σοὶ δ' ὑπίλλουσιν στόμα.

Κρέων
σὺ δ᾽ οὐκ ἐπαιδεῖ, τῶνδε χωρὶς εἰ φρονεῖς;   510

Ἀντιγόνη
οὐδὲν γὰρ αἰσχρὸν τοὺς ὁμοσπλάγχνους σέβειν.

Κρέων
οὔκουν ὅμαιμος χὠ καταντίον θανών;

Ἀντιγόνη
ὅμαιμος ἐκ μιᾶς τε καὶ ταὐτοῦ πατρός.

Κρέων
πῶς δῆτ᾽ ἐκείνῳ δυσσεβῆ τιμᾷς χάριν;

Ἀντιγόνη
οὐ μαρτυρήσει ταῦθ᾽ ὁ κατθανὼν νέκυς.

Κρέων
εἴ τοί σφε τιμᾷς ἐξ ἴσου τῷ δυσσεβεῖ.

Ἀντιγόνη
οὐ γάρ τι δοῦλος, ἀλλ᾽ ἀδελφὸς ὤλετο.

Κρέων
πορθῶν δὲ τήνδε γῆν· ὁ δ᾽ ἀντιστὰς ὕπερ.

Ἀντιγόνη
ὁμῶς ὅ γ' Ἅιδης τοὺς νόμους τούτους ποθεῖ.

Κρέων
ἀλλ' οὐχ ὁ χρηστὸς τῷ κακῷ λαχεῖν ἴσος.   520

Ἀντιγόνη
τίς οἶδεν εἰ κάτωθεν εὐαγῆ τάδε;

Κρέων
οὔτοι ποθ' οὑχθρός, οὐδ' ὅταν θάνῃ, φίλος.

Ἀντιγόνη
οὔτοι συνέχθειν, ἀλλὰ συμφιλεῖν ἔφυν.

Κρέων
κάτω νυν ἐλθοῦσ', εἰ φιλητέον, φίλει
κείνους· ἐμοῦ δὲ ζῶντος οὐκ ἄρξει γυνή.

Χορός
καὶ μὴν πρὸ πυλῶν ἥδ' Ἰσμήνη,
φιλάδελφα κάτω δάκρυ' εἰβομένη·
νεφέλη δ' ὀφρύων ὕπερ αἱματόεν
ῥέθος αἰσχύνει,
τέγγουσ' εὐῶπα παρειάν.   530

Κρέων
σὺ δ', ἣ κατ' οἴκους ὡς ἔχιδν' ὑφειμένη
λήθουσά μ' ἐξέπινες, οὐδ' ἐμάνθανον
τρέφων δύ' ἄτα κἀπαναστάσεις θρόνων,
φέρ', εἰπὲ δή μοι, καὶ σὺ τοῦδε τοῦ τάφου
φήσεις μετασχεῖν, ἢ 'ξομεῖ τὸ μὴ εἰδέναι;

Ἰσμήνη
δέδρακα τοὔργον, εἴπερ ἥδ' ὁμορροθεῖ
καὶ ξυμμετίσχω καὶ φέρω τῆς αἰτίας.

Ἀντιγόνη
ἀλλ' οὐκ ἐάσει τοῦτό γ' ἡ δίκη σ', ἐπεὶ 540
οὔτ' ἠθέλησας οὔτ' ἐγὼ 'κοινωσάμην.

Ἰσμήνη
ἀλλ' ἐν κακοῖς τοῖς σοῖσιν οὐκ αἰσχύνομαι
ξύμπλουν ἐμαυτὴν τοῦ πάθους ποιουμένη.

Ἀντιγόνη
ὧν τοὔργον, Ἅιδης χοἰ κάτω ξυνίστορες·
λόγοις δ' ἐγὼ φιλοῦσαν οὐ στέργω φίλην.

Ἰσμήνη
μήτοι, κασιγνήτη, μ' ἀτιμάσῃς τὸ μὴ οὐ
θανεῖν τε σὺν σοὶ τὸν θανόντα θ' ἁγνίσαι.

Ἀντιγόνη
μή μοι θάνῃς σὺ κοινὰ μηδ' ἃ μὴ 'θιγες
ποιοῦ σεαυτῆς. ἀρκέσω θνῄσκουσ' ἐγώ.

Ἰσμήνη
καὶ τίς βίος μοι σοῦ λελειμμένῃ φίλος;

Ἀντιγόνη
Κρέοντ' ἐρώτα· τοῦδε γὰρ σὺ κηδεμών.

Ἰσμήνη
τί ταῦτ' ἀνιᾷς μ', οὐδὲν ὠφελουμένη; 550

Ἀντιγόνη
ἀλγοῦσα μὲν δῆτ' εἰ γελῶ γ' ἐν σοὶ γελῶ.

Ἰσμήνη
τί δῆτ' ἂν ἀλλὰ νῦν σ' ἔτ' ὠφελοῖμ' ἐγώ;

Ἀντιγόνη
σῶσον σεαυτήν· οὐ φθονῶ σ' ὑπεκφυγεῖν.

Ἰσμήνη
οἴμοι τάλαινα, κἀμπλάκω τοῦ σοῦ μόρου;

Ἀντιγόνη
σὺ μὲν γὰρ εἵλου ζῆν, ἐγὼ δὲ κατθανεῖν.

Ἰσμήνη
ἀλλ' οὐκ ἐπ' ἀρρήτοις γε τοῖς ἐμοῖς λόγοις.

Ἀντιγόνη
καλῶς σὺ μὲν τοῖς, τοῖς δ' ἐγὼ 'δόκουν φρονεῖν.

Ἰσμήνη
καὶ μὴν ἴση νῷν ἐστιν ἡ 'ξαμαρτία.

Ἀντιγόνη
θάρσει: σὺ μὲν ζῇς, ἡ δ' ἐμὴ ψυχὴ πάλαι
τέθνηκεν, ὥστε τοῖς θανοῦσιν ὠφελεῖν.   560

Κρέων
τὼ παῖδε φημὶ τώδε τὴν μὲν ἀρτίως
ἄνουν πεφάνθαι, τὴν δ' ἀφ' οὗ τὰ πρῶτ' ἔφυ.

Ἰσμήνη
οὐ γάρ ποτ', ὦναξ, οὐδ' ὃς ἂν βλάστῃ μένει
νοῦς τοῖς κακῶς πράσσουσιν, ἀλλ' ἐξίσταται.

Κρέων

σοὶ γοῦν, ὅθ' εἵλου σὺν κακοῖς πράσσειν κακά.

Ἰσμήνη
τί γὰρ μόνῃ μοι τῆσδ' ἄτερ βιώσιμον;

Κρέων
ἀλλ' ἥδε μέντοι μὴ λέγ'· οὐ γὰρ ἔστ' ἔτι.

Ἰσμήνη
ἀλλὰ κτενεῖς νυμφεῖα τοῦ σαυτοῦ τέκνου;

Κρέων
ἀρώσιμοι γὰρ χἀτέρων εἰσὶν γύαι.

Ἰσμήνη
οὐχ ὥς γ' ἐκείνῳ τῇδέ τ' ἦν ἡρμοσμένα.   570

Κρέων
κακὰς ἐγὼ γυναῖκας υἱέσι στυγῶ.

Ἀντιγόνη
ὦ φίλταθ' Αἷμον, ὥς σ' ἀτιμάζει πατήρ.

Κρέων
ἄγαν γε λυπεῖς καὶ σὺ καὶ τὸ σὸν λέχος.

Χορός
ἦ γὰρ στερήσεις τῆσδε τὸν σαυτοῦ γόνον;

Κρέων
Ἅιδης ὁ παύσων τούσδε τοὺς γάμους ἔφυ.

Ἀντιγόνη

Χορός
δεδογμέν', ὡς ἔοικε, τήνδε κατθανεῖν.

Κρέων
καὶ σοί γε κἀμοί. μὴ τριβὰς ἔτ', ἀλλά νιν
κομίζετ' εἴσω, δμῶες: ἐκ δὲ τοῦδε χρὴ
γυναῖκας εἶναι τάσδε μηδ' ἀνειμένας.
φεύγουσι γάρ τοι χοἰ θρασεῖς, ὅταν πέλας   580
ἤδη τὸν Ἅιδην εἰσορῶσι τοῦ βίου.

Χορός
εὐδαίμονες οἷσι κακῶν ἄγευστος αἰών.
οἷς γὰρ ἂν σεισθῇ θεόθεν δόμος, ἄτας
οὐδὲν ἐλλείπει γενεᾶς ἐπὶ πλῆθος ἕρπον:
ὅμοιον ὥστε ποντίαις οἶδμα δυσπνόοις ὅταν
Θρῄσσαισιν ἔρεβος ὕφαλον ἐπιδράμῃ πνοαῖς,
κυλίνδει βυσσόθεν κελαινὰν θῖνα καὶ   590
δυσάνεμοι, στόνῳ βρέμουσι δ' ἀντιπλῆγες ἀκταί.

ἀρχαῖα τὰ Λαβδακιδᾶν οἴκων ὁρῶμαι
πήματα φθιτῶν ἐπὶ πήμασι πίπτοντ',
οὐδ' ἀπαλλάσσει γενεὰν γένος, ἀλλ' ἐρείπει
θεῶν τις, οὐδ' ἔχει λύσιν. νῦν γὰρ ἐσχάτας ὕπερ
ῥίζας ὃ τέτατο φάος ἐν Οἰδίπου δόμοις,   600
κατ' αὖ νιν φοινία θεῶν τῶν νερτέρων
ἀμᾷ κόνις λόγου τ' ἄνοια καὶ φρενῶν ἐρινύς.

τεάν, Ζεῦ, δύνασιν τίς ἀνδρῶν ὑπερβασία κατάσχοι;

τὰν οὔθ' ὕπνος αἱρεῖ ποθ' ὁ πάντ' ἀγρεύων,
οὔτε θεῶν ἄκματοι μῆνες, ἀγήρῳ δὲ χρόνῳ
δυνάστας κατέχεις Ὀλύμπου 610
μαρμαρόεσσαν αἴγλαν.
τό τ' ἔπειτα καὶ τὸ μέλλον
καὶ τὸ πρὶν ἐπαρκέσει
νόμος ὅδ', οὐδὲν ἕρπει
θνατῶν βιότῳ πάμπολύ γ' ἐκτὸς ἄτας.

ἁ γὰρ δὴ πολύπλαγκτος ἐλπὶς
πολλοῖς μὲν ὄνασις ἀνδρῶν,
πολλοῖς δ' ἀπάτα κουφονόων ἐρώτων·
εἰδότι δ' οὐδὲν ἕρπει, πρὶν πυρὶ θερμῷ πόδα τις προσαύσῃ.
σοφίᾳ γὰρ ἔκ του κλεινὸν ἔπος πέφανται. 620
τὸ κακὸν δοκεῖν ποτ' ἐσθλὸν τῷδ' ἔμμεν
ὅτῳ φρένας θεὸς ἄγει πρὸς ἄταν·

πράσσει δ' ὀλίγιστον χρόνον ἐκτὸς ἄτας.
ὅδε μὴν Αἵμων, παίδων τῶν σῶν
νέατον γέννημ'· ἆρ' ἀχνύμενος
τάλιδος ἥκει μόρον Ἀντιγόνης,
ἀπάτης λεχέων ὑπεραλγῶν; 630

Κρέων
τάχ' εἰσόμεσθα μάντεων ὑπέρτερον.
ὦ παῖ, τελείαν ψῆφον ἆρα μὴ κλύων
τῆς μελλονύμφου πατρὶ λυσσαίνων πάρει;
ἦ σοὶ μὲν ἡμεῖς πανταχῇ, δρῶντες φίλοι;

Αἵμων
πάτερ, σός εἰμι, καὶ σύ μοι γνώμας ἔχων
χρηστὰς ἀπορθοῖς, αἷς ἔγωγ' ἐφέψομαι.
ἐμοὶ γὰρ οὐδεὶς ἀξιώσεται γάμος
μείζων φέρεσθαι σοῦ καλῶς ἡγουμένου.

Κρέων
οὕτω γάρ, ὦ παῖ, χρὴ διὰ στέρνων ἔχειν,
γνώμης πατρῴας πάντ' ὄπισθεν ἑστάναι. 640
τούτου γὰρ οὕνεκ' ἄνδρες εὔχονται γονὰς
κατηκόους φύσαντες ἐν δόμοις ἔχειν,
ὡς καὶ τὸν ἐχθρὸν ἀνταμύνωνται κακοῖς
καὶ τὸν φίλον τιμῶσιν ἐξ ἴσου πατρί.
ὅστις δ' ἀνωφέλητα φιτύει τέκνα,
τί τόνδ' ἂν εἴποις ἄλλο πλὴν αὑτῷ πόνους
φῦσαι, πολὺν δὲ τοῖσιν ἐχθροῖσιν γέλων;
μή νύν ποτ', ὦ παῖ, τὰς φρένας ὑφ' ἡδονῆς
γυναικὸς οὕνεκ' ἐκβάλῃς, εἰδὼς ὅτι
ψυχρὸν παραγκάλισμα τοῦτο γίγνεται, 650
γυνὴ κακὴ ξύνευνος ἐν δόμοις. τί γὰρ
γένοιτ' ἂν ἕλκος μεῖζον ἢ φίλος κακός;
ἀλλὰ πτύσας ὡσεί τε δυσμενῆ μέθες
τὴν παῖδ' ἐν Ἅιδου τήνδε νυμφεύειν τινί.
ἐπεὶ γὰρ αὐτὴν εἷλον ἐμφανῶς ἐγὼ
πόλεως ἀπιστήσασαν ἐκ πάσης μόνην,
ψευδῆ γ' ἐμαυτὸν οὐ καταστήσω πόλει,
ἀλλὰ κτενῶ. πρὸς ταῦτ' ἐφυμνείτω Δία

ξύναιμον. εἰ γὰρ δὴ τά γ' ἐγγενῆ φύσει
ἄκοσμα θρέψω, κάρτα τοὺς ἔξω γένους. 660
ἐν τοῖς γὰρ οἰκείοισιν ὅστις ἔστ' ἀνὴρ
χρηστός, φανεῖται κἀν πόλει δίκαιος ὤν.
ὅστις δ' ὑπερβὰς ἢ νόμους βιάζεται
ἢ τοὐπιτάσσειν τοῖς κρατύνουσιν νοεῖ,
οὐκ ἔστ' ἐπαίνου τοῦτον ἐξ ἐμοῦ τυχεῖν.
ἀλλ' ὃν πόλις στήσειε τοῦδε χρὴ κλύειν
καὶ σμικρὰ καὶ δίκαια καὶ τἀναντία.
καὶ τοῦτον ἂν τὸν ἄνδρα θαρσοίην ἐγὼ
καλῶς μὲν ἄρχειν, εὖ δ' ἂν ἄρχεσθαι θέλειν,
δορός τ' ἂν ἐν χειμῶνι προστεταγμένον 670
μένειν δίκαιον κἀγαθὸν παραστάτην.
ἀναρχίας δὲ μεῖζον οὐκ ἔστιν κακόν.
αὕτη πόλεις ὄλλυσιν, ἥδ' ἀναστάτους
οἴκους τίθησιν, ἥδε συμμάχου δορὸς
τροπὰς καταρρήγνυσι· τῶν δ' ὀρθουμένων
σῴζει τὰ πολλὰ σώμαθ' ἡ πειθαρχία.
οὕτως ἀμυντέ' ἐστὶ τοῖς κοσμουμένοις,
κοὔτοι γυναικὸς οὐδαμῶς ἡσσητέα.
κρεῖσσον γάρ, εἴπερ δεῖ, πρὸς ἀνδρὸς ἐκπεσεῖν,
κοὐκ ἂν γυναικῶν ἥσσονες καλοίμεθ' ἄν. 680

Χορός
ἡμῖν μέν, εἰ μὴ τῷ χρόνῳ κεκλέμμεθα,
λέγειν φρονούντως ὧν λέγεις δοκεῖς πέρι.

Ἀντιγόνη

Αἵμων
πάτερ, θεοὶ φύουσιν ἀνθρώποις φρένας,
πάντων ὅσ' ἐστὶ κτημάτων ὑπέρτατον.
ἐγὼ δ' ὅπως σὺ μὴ λέγεις ὀρθῶς τάδε,
οὔτ' ἂν δυναίμην μήτ' ἐπισταίμην λέγειν.
γένοιτο μεντἂν χἀτέρῳ καλῶς ἔχον.
σοῦ δ' οὖν πέφυκα πάντα προσκοπεῖν ὅσα
λέγει τις ἢ πράσσει τις ἢ ψέγειν ἔχει.
τὸ γὰρ σὸν ὄμμα δεινὸν, ἀνδρὶ δημότῃ 690
λόγοις τοιούτοις, οἷς σὺ μὴ τέρψει κλύων:
ἐμοὶ δ' ἀκούειν ἔσθ' ὑπὸ σκότου τάδε,
τὴν παῖδα ταύτην οἷ', ὀδύρεται πόλις,
πασῶν γυναικῶν ὡς ἀναξιωτάτη
κάκιστ' ἀπ' ἔργων εὐκλεεστάτων φθίνει.
ἥτις τὸν αὑτῆς αὐτάδελφον ἐν φοναῖς
πεπτῶτ' ἄθαπτον μήθ' ὑπ' ὠμηστῶν κυνῶν
εἴασ' ὀλέσθαι μήθ' ὑπ' οἰωνῶν τινος.
οὐχ ἥδε χρυσῆς ἀξία τιμῆς λαχεῖν;
τοιάδ' ἐρεμνὴ σῖγ' ἐπέρχεται φάτις. 700
ἐμοὶ δὲ σοῦ πράσσοντος εὐτυχῶς, πάτερ,
οὐκ ἔστιν οὐδὲν κτῆμα τιμιώτερον,
τί γὰρ πατρὸς θάλλοντος εὐκλείας τέκνοις
ἄγαλμα μεῖζον, ἢ τί πρὸς παίδων πατρί;
μή νυν ἓν ἦθος μοῦνον ἐν σαυτῷ φόρει,
ὡς φῂς σύ, κοὐδὲν ἄλλο, τοῦτ' ὀρθῶς ἔχειν.
ὅστις γὰρ αὐτὸς ἢ φρονεῖν μόνος δοκεῖ,
ἢ γλῶσσαν, ἣν οὐκ ἄλλος, ἢ ψυχὴν ἔχειν,
οὗτοι διαπτυχθέντες ὤφθησαν κενοί.

ἀλλ' ἄνδρα, κεἴ τις ᾖ σοφός, τὸ μανθάνειν 710
πόλλ', αἰσχρὸν οὐδὲν καὶ τὸ μὴ τείνειν ἄγαν.
ὁρᾷς παρὰ ῥείθροισι χειμάρροις ὅσα
δένδρων ὑπείκει, κλῶνας ὡς ἐκσῴζεται,
τὰ δ' ἀντιτείνοντ' αὐτόπρεμν' ἀπόλλυται.
αὔτως δὲ ναὸς ὅστις ἐγκρατῆ πόδα
τείνας ὑπείκει μηδέν, ὑπτίοις κάτω
στρέψας τὸ λοιπὸν σέλμασιν ναυτίλλεται.
ἀλλ' εἶκε καὶ θυμῷ μετάστασιν δίδου.
γνώμη γὰρ εἴ τις κἀπ' ἐμοῦ νεωτέρου
πρόσεστι, φήμ' ἔγωγε πρεσβεύειν πολὺ 720
φῦναι τὸν ἄνδρα πάντ' ἐπιστήμης πλέων·
εἰ δ' οὖν, φιλεῖ γὰρ τοῦτο μὴ ταύτῃ ῥέπειν,
καὶ τῶν λεγόντων εὖ καλὸν τὸ μανθάνειν.

Χορός
ἄναξ, σέ τ' εἰκός, εἴ τι καίριον λέγει,
μαθεῖν, σέ τ' αὖ τοῦδ'· εὖ γὰρ εἴρηται διπλῇ.

Κρέων
οἱ τηλικοίδε καὶ διδαξόμεσθα δὴ
φρονεῖν ὑπ' ἀνδρὸς τηλικοῦδε τὴν φύσιν;

Αἵμων
μηδὲν τὸ μὴ δίκαιον· εἰ δ' ἐγὼ νέος,
οὐ τὸν χρόνον χρὴ μᾶλλον ἢ τἄργα σκοπεῖν.

Κρέων
ἔργον γάρ ἐστι τοὺς ἀκοσμοῦντας σέβειν; 730

Αἵμων
οὐδ' ἂν κελεύσαιμ', εὐσεβεῖν εἰς τοὺς κακούς.

Κρέων
οὐχ ἥδε γὰρ τοιᾷδ' ἐπείληπται νόσῳ;

Αἵμων
οὔ φησι Θήβης τῆσδ' ὁμόπτολις λεώς.

Κρέων
πόλις γὰρ ἡμῖν ἁμὲ χρὴ τάσσειν ἐρεῖ;

Αἵμων
ὁρᾷς τόδ' ὡς εἴρηκας ὡς ἄγαν νέος;

Κρέων
ἄλλῳ γὰρ ἢ 'μοὶ χρή με τῆσδ' ἄρχειν χθονός;

Αἵμων
πόλις γὰρ οὐκ ἔσθ' ἥτις ἀνδρός ἐσθ' ἑνός.

Κρέων
οὐ τοῦ κρατοῦντος ἡ πόλις νομίζεται;

Αἵμων
καλῶς γ' ἐρήμης ἂν σὺ γῆς ἄρχοις μόνος.

Κρέων
ὅδ', ὡς ἔοικε, τῇ γυναικὶ συμμαχεῖ.   740

Αἵμων
εἴπερ γυνὴ σύ. σοῦ γὰρ οὖν προκήδομαι.

Κρέων
ὦ παγκάκιστε, διὰ δίκης ἰὼν πατρί;

Αἵμων
οὐ γὰρ δίκαιά σ' ἐξαμαρτάνονθ' ὁρῶ.

Κρέων
ἁμαρτάνω γὰρ τὰς ἐμὰς ἀρχὰς σέβων;

Αἵμων
οὐ γὰρ σέβεις τιμάς γε τὰς θεῶν πατῶν.

Κρέων
ὦ μιαρὸν ἦθος καὶ γυναικὸς ὕστερον.

Αἵμων
οὔ τἂν ἕλοις ἥσσω γε τῶν αἰσχρῶν ἐμέ.

Κρέων
ὁ γοῦν λόγος σοι πᾶς ὑπὲρ κείνης ὅδε.

Αἵμων
καὶ σοῦ γε κἀμοῦ, καὶ θεῶν τῶν νερτέρων.

Κρέων
ταύτην ποτ' οὐκ ἔσθ' ὡς ἔτι ζῶσαν γαμεῖς. 750

Αἵμων
ἣ δ' οὖν θανεῖται καὶ θανοῦσ' ὀλεῖ τινα.

Κρέων
ἦ κἀπαπειλῶν ὧδ' ἐπεξέρχει θρασύς;

Αἵμων
τίς δ' ἔστ' ἀπειλὴ πρὸς κενὰς γνώμας λέγειν;

Κρέων
κλαίων φρενώσεις, ὢν φρενῶν αὐτὸς κενός.

Αἵμων
εἰ μὴ πατὴρ ἦσθ', εἶπον ἄν σ' οὐκ εὖ φρονεῖν.

Κρέων
γυναικὸς ὢν δούλευμα μὴ κώτιλλέ με.

Αἵμων
βούλει λέγειν τι καὶ λέγων μηδὲν κλύειν;

Κρέων
ἄληθες; ἀλλ' οὐ τόνδ' Ὄλυμπον, ἴσθ' ὅτι,
χαίρων ἐπὶ ψόγοισι δεννάσεις ἐμέ.
ἄγαγε τὸ μῖσος ὡς κατ' ὄμματ' αὐτίκα 760
παρόντι θνῄσκῃ πλησία τῷ νυμφίῳ.

Αἵμων
οὐ δῆτ' ἔμοιγε, τοῦτο μὴ δόξῃς ποτέ,
οὔθ' ἥδ' ὀλεῖται πλησία, σύ τ' οὐδαμὰ
τοὐμὸν προσόψει κρᾶτ' ἐν ὀφθαλμοῖς ὁρῶν,
ὡς τοῖς θέλουσι τῶν φίλων μαίνῃ συνών.

Χορός
ἁνήρ, ἄναξ, βέβηκεν ἐξ ὀργῆς ταχύς·
νοῦς δ' ἐστὶ τηλικοῦτος ἀλγήσας βαρύς.

Κρέων
δράτω· φρονείτω μεῖζον ἢ κατ' ἄνδρ' ἰών·
τὼ δ' οὖν κόρα τώδ' οὐκ ἀπαλλάξει μόρου.

Χορός
ἄμφω γὰρ αὐτὼ καὶ κατακτεῖναι νοεῖς; 770

Κρέων
οὐ τήν γε μὴ θιγοῦσαν· εὖ γὰρ οὖν λέγεις.

Χορός
μόρῳ δὲ ποίῳ καί σφε βουλεύει κτανεῖν;

Κρέων
ἄγων ἔρημος ἔνθ' ἂν ᾖ βροτῶν στίβος
κρύψω πετρώδει ζῶσαν ἐν κατώρυχι,
φορβῆς τοσοῦτον ὡς ἄγος μόνον προθείς,
ὅπως μίασμα πᾶσ' ὑπεκφύγῃ πόλις.
κἀκεῖ τὸν Ἅιδην, ὃν μόνον σέβει θεῶν,
αἰτουμένη που τεύξεται τὸ μὴ θανεῖν,
ἢ γνώσεται γοῦν ἀλλὰ τηνικαῦθ' ὅτι
πόνος περισσός ἐστι τὰν Ἅιδου σέβειν.   780

Χορός
Ἔρως ἀνίκατε μάχαν,
Ἔρως, ὃς ἐν κτήμασι πίπτεις,
ὃς ἐν μαλακαῖς παρειαῖς νεάνιδος ἐννυχεύεις,
φοιτᾷς δ' ὑπερπόντιος ἔν τ' ἀγρονόμοις αὐλαῖς·
καί σ' οὔτ' ἀθανάτων φύξιμος οὐδεὶς
οὔθ' ἀμερίων σέ γ' ἀνθρώπων.
ὁ δ' ἔχων μέμηνεν.   790

σὺ καὶ δικαίων ἀδίκους φρένας παρασπᾷς ἐπὶ λώβᾳ,
σὺ καὶ τόδε νεῖκος ἀνδρῶν ξύναιμον ἔχεις ταράξας·
νικᾷ δ' ἐναργὴς βλεφάρων ἵμερος εὐλέκτρου

νύμφας, τῶν μεγάλων πάρεδρος ἐν ἀρχαῖς
θεσμῶν. ἄμαχος γὰρ ἐμπαίζει θεὸς, Ἀφροδίτα.   800

νῦν δ' ἤδη 'γὼ καὐτὸς θεσμῶν
ἔξω φέρομαι τάδ' ὁρῶν ἴσχειν δ'
οὐκέτι πηγὰς δύναμαι δάκρυ
τὸν παγκοίτην ὅθ' ὁρῶ θάλαμον
τήνδ' Ἀντιγόνην ἀνύτουσαν.

Ἀντιγόνη
ὁρᾶτ' ἔμ', ὦ γᾶς πατρίας πολῖται, τὰν νεάταν ὁδὸν
στείχουσαν, νέατον δὲ φέγγος λεύσσουσαν ἀελίου,
κοὔποτ' αὖθις. ἀλλά μ' ὁ παγκοίτας Ἅιδας   810
ζῶσαν ἄγει
τὰν Ἀχέροντος
ἀκτάν, οὔθ' ὑμεναίων ἔγκληρον, οὔτ' ἐπινύμφειός
πώ μέ τις ὕμνος ὕμνησεν, ἀλλ' Ἀχέροντι νυμφεύσω.

Χορός
οὔκουν κλεινὴ καὶ ἔπαινον ἔχουσ'
ἐς τόδ' ἀπέρχει κεῦθος νεκύων,
οὔτε φθινάσιν πληγεῖσα νόσοις
οὔτε ξιφέων ἐπίχειρα λαχοῦσ',   820
ἀλλ' αὐτόνομος ζῶσα μόνη δὴ
θνητῶν Ἅιδην καταβήσει.

Ἀντιγόνη
ἤκουσα δὴ λυγρότατον ὀλέσθαι τὰν Φρυγίαν ξέναν

Ταντάλου Σιπύλῳ πρὸς ἄκρῳ, τὰν κισσὸς ὡς ἀτενὴς
πετραία βλάστα δάμασεν, καί νιν ὄμβροι τακομέναν,
ὡς φάτις ἀνδρῶν,
χιών τ' οὐδαμὰ λείπει, 830
τέγγει δ' ὑπ' ὀφρύσι παγκλαύτοις δειράδας·
ᾇ με δαίμων ὁμοιοτάταν κατευνάζει.

Χορός
ἀλλὰ θεός τοι καὶ θεογεννής,
ἡμεῖς δὲ βροτοὶ καὶ θνητογενεῖς.
καίτοι φθιμένῃ μέγα κἀκοῦσαι
τοῖς ἰσοθέοις σύγκληρα λαχεῖν.
ζῶσαν καὶ ἔπειτα θανοῦσαν.

Ἀντιγόνη
οἴμοι γελῶμαι. τί με, πρὸς θεῶν πατρῴων,
οὐκ οἰχομέναν ὑβρίζεις, ἀλλ' ἐπίφαντον; 840
ὦ πόλις, ὦ πόλεως πολυκτήμονες ἄνδρες·
ἰὼ Διρκαῖαι κρῆναι
Θήβας τ' εὐαρμάτου ἄλσος,
ἔμπας ξυμμάρτυρας ὔμμ' ἐπικτῶμαι,
οἵα φίλων ἄκλαυτος, οἵοις νόμοις
πρὸς ἔργμα τυμβόχωστον ἔρχομαι τάφου ποταινίου·
ἰὼ δύστανος, βροτοῖς οὔτε νεκροῖς κυροῦσα 850
μέτοικος οὐ ζῶσιν, οὐ θανοῦσιν.

Χορός
προβᾶσ' ἐπ' ἔσχατον θράσους

ὑψηλὸν ἐς Δίκας βάθρον
προσέπεσες, ὦ τέκνον, πολύ·
πατρῷον δ' ἐκτίνεις τιν' ἆθλον.

Ἀντιγόνη
ἔψαυσας ἀλγεινοτάτας ἐμοὶ μερίμνας,
πατρὸς τριπόλιστον οἶκτον τοῦ τε πρόπαντος
ἁμετέρου πότμου κλεινοῖς Λαβδακίδαισιν.   860
ἰὼ ματρῷαι λέκτρων
ἆται κοιμήματά τ' αὐτογέννητ' ἐμῷ πατρὶ δυσμόρου
ματρός,
οἵων ἐγώ ποθ' ἁ ταλαίφρων ἔφυν·
πρὸς οὓς ἀραῖος ἄγαμος ἅδ' ἐγὼ μέτοικος ἔρχομαι.
ἰὼ δυσπότμων κασίγνητε γάμων κυρήσας,   870
θανὼν ἔτ' οὖσαν κατήναρές με.

Χορός
σέβειν μὲν εὐσέβειά τις,
κράτος δ' ὅτῳ κράτος μέλει
παραβατὸν οὐδαμᾷ πέλει·
σὲ δ' αὐτόγνωτος ὤλεσ' ὀργά.

Ἀντιγόνη
ἄκλαυτος, ἄφιλος, ἀνυμέναιος ταλαίφρων ἄγομαι
τὰν πυμάταν ὁδόν. οὐκέτι μοι τόδε
λαμπάδος ἱερὸν ὄμμα
θέμις ὁρᾶν ταλαίνᾳ.   880
τὸν δ' ἐμὸν πότμον ἀδάκρυτον

οὐδεὶς φίλων στενάζει.

Κρέων
ἆρ' ἴστ', ἀοιδὰς καὶ γόους πρὸ τοῦ θανεῖν
ὡς οὐδ' ἂν εἷς παύσαιτ' ἄν, εἰ χρείη λέγειν;
οὐκ ἄξεθ' ὡς τάχιστα; καὶ κατηρεφεῖ
τύμβῳ περιπτύξαντες, ὡς εἴρηκ' ἐγώ,
ἄφετε μόνην ἔρημον, εἴτε χρῇ θανεῖν
εἴτ' ἐν τοιαύτῃ ζῶσα τυμβεύειν στέγῃ·
ἡμεῖς γὰρ ἁγνοὶ τοὐπὶ τήνδε τὴν κόρην·
μετοικίας δ' οὖν τῆς ἄνω στερήσεται. 890

Ἀντιγόνη
ὦ τύμβος, ὦ νυμφεῖον, ὦ κατασκαφὴς
οἴκησις ἀείφρουρος, οἷ πορεύομαι
πρὸς τοὺς ἐμαυτῆς, ὧν ἀριθμὸν ἐν νεκροῖς
πλεῖστον δέδεκται Φερσέφασσ' ὀλωλότων·
ὧν λοισθία 'γὼ καὶ κάκιστα δὴ μακρῷ
κάτειμι, πρίν μοι μοῖραν ἐξήκειν βίου.
ἐλθοῦσα μέντοι κάρτ' ἐν ἐλπίσιν τρέφω
φίλη μὲν ἥξειν πατρί, προσφιλὴς δὲ σοί,
μῆτερ, φίλη δὲ σοί, κασίγνητον κάρα·
ἐπεὶ θανόντας αὐτόχειρ ὑμᾶς ἐγὼ 900
ἔλουσα κἀκόσμησα κἀπιτυμβίους
χοὰς ἔδωκα. νῦν δέ Πολύνεικες, τὸ σὸν
δέμας περιστέλλουσα τοιάδ' ἄρνυμαι.
καίτοι σ' ἐγὼ 'τίμησα τοῖς φρονοῦσιν εὖ.
οὐ γάρ ποτ' οὔτ' ἄν, εἰ τέκνων μήτηρ ἔφυν,

οὔτ' εἰ πόσις μοι κατθανὼν ἐτήκετο,
βίᾳ πολιτῶν τόνδ' ἂν ᾐρόμην πόνον.
τίνος νόμου δὴ ταῦτα πρὸς χάριν λέγω;
πόσις μὲν ἄν μοι κατθανόντος ἄλλος ἦν,
καὶ παῖς ἀπ' ἄλλου φωτός, εἰ τοῦδ' ἤμπλακον, 910
μητρὸς δ' ἐν Ἅιδου καὶ πατρὸς κεκευθότοιν
οὐκ ἔστ' ἀδελφὸς ὅστις ἂν βλάστοι ποτέ.
τοιῷδε μέντοι σ' ἐκπροτιμήσασ' ἐγὼ
νόμῳ Κρέοντι ταῦτ' ἔδοξ' ἁμαρτάνειν
καὶ δεινὰ τολμᾶν, ὦ κασίγνητον κάρα.
καὶ νῦν ἄγει με διὰ χερῶν οὕτω λαβὼν
ἄλεκτρον, ἀνυμέναιον, οὔτε του γάμου
μέρος λαχοῦσαν οὔτε παιδείου τροφῆς,
ἀλλ' ὧδ' ἔρημος πρὸς φίλων ἡ δύσμορος
ζῶσ' εἰς θανόντων ἔρχομαι κατασκαφάς. 920
ποίαν παρεξελθοῦσα δαιμόνων δίκην;
τί χρή με τὴν δύστηνον ἐς θεοὺς ἔτι
βλέπειν; τίν' αὐδᾶν ξυμμάχων; ἐπεί γε δὴ
τὴν δυσσέβειαν εὐσεβοῦσ', ἐκτησάμην.
ἀλλ' εἰ μὲν οὖν τάδ' ἐστὶν ἐν θεοῖς καλά,
παθόντες ἂν ξυγγνοῖμεν ἡμαρτηκότες·
εἰ δ' οἵδ' ἁμαρτάνουσι, μὴ πλείω κακὰ
πάθοιεν ἢ καὶ δρῶσιν ἐκδίκως ἐμέ.

Χορός
ἔτι τῶν αὐτῶν ἀνέμων αὐταὶ
ψυχῆς ῥιπαὶ τήνδε γ' ἔχουσιν. 930

Κρέων
τοιγὰρ τούτων τοῖσιν ἄγουσιν
κλαύμαθ' ὑπάρξει βραδυτῆτος ὕπερ.

Ἀντιγόνη
οἴμοι, θανάτου τοῦτ' ἐγγυτάτω
τοὔπος ἀφῖκται.

Χορός
θαρσεῖν οὐδὲν παραμυθοῦμαι
μὴ οὐ τάδε ταύτῃ κατακυροῦσθαι.

Ἀντιγόνη
ὦ γῆς Θήβης ἄστυ πατρῷον
καὶ θεοὶ προγενεῖς,
ἄγομαι δὴ κοὐκέτι μέλλω.
λεύσσετε, Θήβης οἱ κοιρανίδαι   940
τὴν βασιλειδᾶν μούνην λοιπήν,
οἷα πρὸς οἵων ἀνδρῶν πάσχω,
τὴν εὐσεβίαν σεβίσασα.

Χορός
ἔτλα καὶ Δανάας οὐράνιον φῶς
ἀλλάξαι δέμας ἐν χαλκοδέτοις αὐλαῖς·
κρυπτομένα δ' ἐν τυμβήρει θαλάμῳ κατεζεύχθη·
καίτοι καὶ γενεᾷ τίμιος, ὦ παῖ παῖ,
καὶ Ζηνὸς ταμιεύεσκε γονὰς χρυσορύτους.   950
ἀλλ' ἁ μοιριδία τις δύνασις δεινά·

οὔτ' ἄν νιν ὄλβος οὔτ' Ἄρης, οὐ πύργος, οὐχ ἁλίκτυποι
κελαιναὶ νᾶες ἐκφύγοιεν.

ζεύχθη δ' ὀξύχολος παῖς ὁ Δρύαντος,
Ἠδωνῶν βασιλεύς, κερτομίοις ὀργαῖς
ἐκ Διονύσου πετρώδει κατάφαρκτος ἐν δεσμῷ.
οὕτω τᾶς μανίας δεινὸν ἀποστάζει
ἀνθηρόν τε μένος. κεῖνος ἐπέγνω μανίαις   960
ψαύων τὸν θεὸν ἐν κερτομίοις γλώσσαις.
παύεσκε μὲν γὰρ ἐνθέους γυναῖκας εὔιόν τε πῦρ,
φιλαύλους τ' ἠρέθιζε Μούσας.

παρὰ δὲ κυανεᾶν πελάγει διδύμας ἁλὸς
ἀκταὶ Βοσπόριαι ἠδ' ὁ Θρηκῶν ἄξενος
Σαλμυδησσός, ἵν' ἀγχίπτολις Ἄρης   970
δισσοῖσι Φινείδαις
εἶδεν ἀρατὸν ἕλκος
τυφλωθὲν ἐξ ἀγρίας δάμαρτος
ἀλαὸν ἀλαστόροισιν ὀμμάτων κύκλοις
ἀραχθέντων, ὑφ' αἱματηραῖς
χείρεσσι καὶ κερκίδων ἀκμαῖσιν.

κατὰ δὲ τακόμενοι μέλεοι μελέαν πάθαν
κλαῖον, ματρὸς ἔχοντες ἀνύμφευτον γονάν·   980
ἁ δὲ σπέρμα μὲν ἀρχαιογόνων
ἄντασ' Ἐρεχθειδᾶν,
τηλεπόροις δ' ἐν ἄντροις

τράφη θυέλλαισιν ἐν πατρῴαις
Βορεὰς ἄμιππος ὀρθόποδος ὑπὲρ πάγου
θεῶν παῖς. ἀλλὰ κἀπ' ἐκείνᾳ
Μοῖραι μακραίωνες ἔσχον, ὦ παῖ.

Τειρεσίας
Θήβης ἄνακτες, ἥκομεν κοινὴν ὁδὸν
δύ' ἐξ ἑνὸς βλέποντε: τοῖς τυφλοῖσι γὰρ
αὕτη κέλευθος ἐκ προηγητοῦ πέλει. 990

Κρέων
τί δ' ἔστιν, ὦ γεραιὲ Τειρεσία, νέον;

Τειρεσίας
ἐγὼ διδάξω, καὶ σὺ τῷ μάντει πιθοῦ.

Κρέων
οὔκουν πάρος γε σῆς ἀπεστάτουν φρενός.

Τειρεσίας
τοιγὰρ δι' ὀρθῆς τήνδ' ἐναυκλήρεις πόλιν.

Κρέων
ἔχω πεπονθὼς μαρτυρεῖν ὀνήσιμα.

Τειρεσίας
φρόνει βεβὼς αὖ νῦν ἐπὶ ξυροῦ τύχης.

Κρέων
τί δ' ἔστιν; ὡς ἐγὼ τὸ σὸν φρίσσω στόμα.

Τειρεσίας
γνώσει, τέχνης σημεῖα τῆς ἐμῆς κλύων.
εἰς γὰρ παλαιὸν θᾶκον ὀρνιθοσκόπον
ἵζων, ἵν' ἦν μοι παντὸς οἰωνοῦ λιμήν, 1000
ἀγνῶτ' ἀκούω φθόγγον ὀρνίθων, κακῷ
κλάζοντας οἴστρῳ καὶ βεβαρβαρωμένῳ.
καὶ σπῶντας ἐν χηλαῖσιν ἀλλήλους φοναῖς
ἔγνων· πτερῶν γὰρ ῥοῖβδος οὐκ ἄσημος ἦν.
εὐθὺς δὲ δείσας ἐμπύρων ἐγευόμην
βωμοῖσι παμφλέκτοισιν· ἐκ δὲ θυμάτων
Ἥφαιστος οὐκ ἔλαμπεν, ἀλλ' ἐπὶ σποδῷ
μυδῶσα κηκὶς μηρίων ἐτήκετο
κἄτυφε κἀνέπτυε, καὶ μετάρσιοι
χολαὶ διεσπείροντο, καὶ καταρρυεῖς 1010
μηροὶ καλυπτῆς ἐξέκειντο πιμελῆς.
τοιαῦτα παιδὸς τοῦδ' ἐμάνθανον πάρα,
φθίνοντ' ἀσήμων ὀργίων μαντεύματα.
ἐμοὶ γὰρ οὗτος ἡγεμών, ἄλλοις δ' ἐγώ.
καὶ ταῦτα τῆς σῆς ἐκ φρενὸς νοσεῖ πόλις.
βωμοὶ γὰρ ἡμῖν ἐσχάραι τε παντελεῖς
πλήρεις ὑπ' οἰωνῶν τε καὶ κυνῶν βορᾶς
τοῦ δυσμόρου πεπτῶτος Οἰδίπου γόνου.
κᾆτ' οὐ δέχονται θυστάδας λιτὰς ἔτι
θεοὶ παρ' ἡμῶν οὐδὲ μηρίων φλόγα, 1020

οὐδ' ὄρνις εὐσήμους ἀπορροιβδεῖ βοάς
ἀνδροφθόρου βεβρῶτες αἵματος λίπος.
ταῦτ' οὖν, τέκνον, φρόνησον. ἀνθρώποισι γὰρ
τοῖς πᾶσι κοινόν ἐστι τοὐξαμαρτάνειν·
ἐπεὶ δ' ἁμάρτῃ, κεῖνος οὐκέτ' ἔστ' ἀνὴρ
ἄβουλος οὐδ' ἄνολβος, ὅστις ἐς κακὸν
πεσὼν ἀκῆται μηδ' ἀκίνητος πέλῃ.
αὐθαδία τοι σκαιότητ' ὀφλισκάνει.
ἀλλ' εἶκε τῷ θανόντι μηδ' ὀλωλότα
κέντει· τίς ἀλκὴ τὸν θανόντ' ἐπικτανεῖν; 1030
εὖ σοι φρονήσας εὖ λέγω. τὸ μανθάνειν δ'
ἥδιστον εὖ λέγοντος, εἰ κέρδος λέγοι.

Κρέων
ὦ πρέσβυ, πάντες ὥστε τοξόται σκοποῦ
τοξεύετ' ἀνδρὸς τοῦδε, κοὐδὲ μαντικῆς
ἄπρακτος ὑμῖν εἰμι· τῶν δ' ὑπαὶ γένους
ἐξημπόλημαι κἀμπεφόρτισμαι πάλαι.
κερδαίνετ', ἐμπολᾶτε τἀπὸ Σάρδεων
ἤλεκτρον, εἰ βούλεσθε, καὶ τὸν Ἰνδικὸν
χρυσόν· τάφῳ δ' ἐκεῖνον οὐχὶ κρύψετε,
οὐδ' εἰ θέλουσ', οἱ Ζηνὸς αἰετοὶ βορὰν
φέρειν νιν ἁρπάζοντες ἐς Διὸς θρόνους,
οὐδ' ὣς μίασμα τοῦτο μὴ τρέσας ἐγὼ 1040
θάπτειν παρήσω κεῖνον· εὖ γὰρ οἶδ' ὅτι
θεοὺς μιαίνειν οὔτις ἀνθρώπων σθένει.
πίπτουσι δ', ὦ γεραιὲ Τειρεσία, βροτῶν
χοἰ πολλὰ δεινοὶ πτώματ' αἴσχρ', ὅταν λόγους

αἰσχροὺς καλῶς λέγωσι τοῦ κέρδους χάριν.

Τειρεσίας
φεῦ. ἆρ' οἶδεν ἀνθρώπων τις, ἆρα φράζεται,

Κρέων
τί χρῆμα; ποῖον τοῦτο πάγκοινον λέγεις;

Τειρεσίας
ὅσῳ κράτιστον κτημάτων εὐβουλία; 1050

Κρέων
ὅσῳπερ, οἶμαι, μὴ φρονεῖν πλείστη βλάβη.

Τειρεσίας
ταύτης σὺ μέντοι τῆς νόσου πλήρης ἔφυς.

Κρέων
οὐ βούλομαι τὸν μάντιν ἀντειπεῖν κακῶς.

Τειρεσίας
καὶ μὴν λέγεις, ψευδῆ με θεσπίζειν λέγων.

Κρέων
τὸ μαντικὸν γὰρ πᾶν φιλάργυρον γένος.

Τειρεσίας
τὸ δ' ἐκ τυράννων αἰσχροκέρδειαν φιλεῖ.

Κρέων
ἆρ' οἶσθα ταγοὺς ὄντας ἂν λέγῃς λέγων;

Τειρεσίας
οἶδ': ἐξ ἐμοῦ γὰρ τήνδ' ἔχεις σώσας πόλιν.

Κρέων
σοφὸς σὺ μάντις, ἀλλὰ τἀδικεῖν φιλῶν.

Τειρεσίας
ὄρσεις με τἀκίνητα διὰ φρενῶν φράσαι. 1060

Κρέων
κίνει, μόνον δὲ μὴ 'πὶ κέρδεσιν λέγων.

Τειρεσίας
οὕτω γὰρ ἤδη καὶ δοκῶ τὸ σὸν μέρος.

Κρέων
ὡς μὴ 'μπολήσων ἴσθι τὴν ἐμὴν φρένα.

Τειρεσίας
ἀλλ' εὖ γέ τοι κάτισθι μὴ πολλοὺς ἔτι
τρόχους ἁμιλλητῆρας ἡλίου τελεῖν,

ἐν οἷσι τῶν σῶν αὐτὸς ἐκ σπλάγχνων ἕνα
νέκυν νεκρῶν ἀμοιβὸν ἀντιδοὺς ἔσει,
ἀνθ' ὧν ἔχεις μὲν τῶν ἄνω βαλὼν κάτω
ψυχήν τ' ἀτίμως ἐν τάφῳ κατῴκισας,
ἔχεις δὲ τῶν κάτωθεν ἐνθάδ' αὖ θεῶν   1070
ἄμοιρον, ἀκτέριστον, ἀνόσιον νέκυν.
ὧν οὔτε σοὶ μέτεστιν οὔτε τοῖς ἄνω
θεοῖσιν, ἀλλ' ἐκ σοῦ βιάζονται τάδε.
τούτων σε λωβητῆρες ὑστεροφθόροι
λοχῶσιν Ἅιδου καὶ θεῶν Ἐρινύες,
ἐν τοῖσιν αὐτοῖς τοῖσδε ληφθῆναι κακοῖς.
καὶ ταῦτ' ἄθρησον εἰ κατηργυρωμένος
λέγω: φανεῖ γὰρ οὐ μακροῦ χρόνου τριβὴ
ἀνδρῶν γυναικῶν σοῖς δόμοις κωκύματα.
ἐχθραὶ δὲ πᾶσαι συνταράσσονται πόλεις,   1080
ὅσων σπαράγματ' ἢ κύνες καθήγνισαν
ἢ θῆρες ἤ τις πτηνὸς οἰωνός, φέρων
ἀνόσιον ὀσμὴν ἑστιοῦχον ἐς πόλιν.
τοιαῦτά σου, λυπεῖς γάρ, ὥστε τοξότης
ἀφῆκα θυμῷ, καρδίας τοξεύματα
βέβαια, τῶν σὺ θάλπος οὐχ ὑπεκδραμεῖ.
ὦ παῖ, σὺ δ' ἡμᾶς ἄπαγε πρὸς δόμους, ἵνα
τὸν θυμὸν οὗτος ἐς νεωτέρους ἀφῇ,
καὶ γνῷ τρέφειν τὴν γλῶσσαν ἡσυχαιτέραν
τὸν νοῦν τ' ἀμείνω τῶν φρενῶν ἢ νῦν φέρει.   1090

Χορός
ἀνήρ, ἄναξ, βέβηκε δεινὰ θεσπίσας:

ἐπιστάμεσθα δ', ἐξ ὅτου λευκὴν ἐγὼ
τήνδ' ἐκ μελαίνης ἀμφιβάλλομαι τρίχα,
μή πώ ποτ' αὐτὸν ψεῦδος ἐς πόλιν λακεῖν.

Κρέων
ἔγνωκα καὐτὸς καὶ ταράσσομαι φρένας.
τό τ' εἰκαθεῖν γὰρ δεινόν, ἀντιστάντα δὲ
ἄτῃ πατάξαι θυμὸν ἐν δεινῷ πάρα.

Χορός
εὐβουλίας δεῖ, παῖ Μενοικέως, λαβεῖν.

Κρέων
τί δῆτα χρὴ δρᾶν; φράζε. πείσομαι δ' ἐγώ.

Χορός
ἐλθὼν κόρην μὲν ἐκ κατώρυχος στέγης   1100
ἄνες, κτίσον δὲ τῷ προκειμένῳ, τάφον.

Κρέων
καὶ ταῦτ' ἐπαινεῖς καὶ δοκεῖς παρεικαθεῖν;

Χορός
ὅσον γ', ἄναξ, τάχιστα: συντέμνουσι γὰρ
θεῶν ποδώκεις τοὺς κακόφρονας βλάβαι.

Κρέων
οἴμοι· μόλις μέν, καρδίας δ' ἐξίσταμαι
τὸ δρᾶν· ἀνάγκῃ δ' οὐχὶ δυσμαχητέον.

Χορός
δρᾶ νυν τάδ' ἐλθὼν μηδ' ἐπ' ἄλλοισιν τρέπε.

Κρέων
ὧδ' ὡς ἔχω στείχοιμ' ἄν· ἴτ' ἴτ' ὀπάονες,
οἵ τ' ὄντες οἵ τ' ἀπόντες, ἀξίνας χεροῖν
ὁρμᾶσθ' ἑλόντες εἰς ἐπόψιον τόπον.   1110
ἐγὼ δ', ἐπειδὴ δόξα τῇδ' ἐπεστράφη,
αὐτός τ' ἔδησα καὶ παρὼν ἐκλύσομαι.
δέδοικα γὰρ μὴ τοὺς καθεστῶτας νόμους
ἄριστον ᾖ σώζοντα τὸν βίον τελεῖν.

Χορός
πολυώνυμε, Καδμείας νύμφας ἄγαλμα
καὶ Διὸς βαρυβρεμέτα
γένος, κλυτὰν ὃς ἀμφέπεις
Ἰταλίαν, μέδεις δὲ
παγκοίνοις, Ἐλευσινίας
Δῃοῦς ἐν κόλποις, Βακχεῦ Βακχᾶν   1120
ὁ ματρόπολιν Θήβαν
ναιετῶν παρ' ὑγρῶν
Ἰσμηνοῦ ῥείθρων ἀγρίου
τ' ἐπὶ σπορᾷ
δράκοντος

σὲ δ' ὑπὲρ διλόφου πέτρας στέροψ ὄπωπε
λιγνύς, ἔνθα Κωρύκιαι
στείχουσι νύμφαι Βακχίδες,
Κασταλίας τε νᾶμα. 1130
καί σε Νυσαίων ὀρέων
κισσήρεις ὄχθαι χλωρά τ' ἀκτὰ
πολυστάφυλος πέμπει,
ἀμβρότων ἐπέων
εὐαζόντων Θηβαίας
ἐπισκοποῦντ' ἀγυιάς·

τὰν ἐκ πᾶσαι τιμᾷς
ὑπερτάταν πόλεων
ματρὶ σὺν κεραυνίᾳ·
καὶ νῦν, ὡς βιαίας ἔχεται 1140
πάνδαμος πόλις ἐπὶ νόσου,
μολεῖν καθαρσίῳ ποδὶ
Παρνασίαν ὑπὲρ κλιτὺν
ἢ στονόεντα πορθμόν.

ἰὼ πῦρ πνειόντων χοράγ' ἄστρων,
Νυχίων φθεγμάτων ἐπίσκοπε,
παῖ Διὸς γένεθλον, προφάνηθ'
ὦναξ, σαῖς ἅμα περιπόλοις 1150
Θυίαισιν, αἵ σε μαινόμεναι πάννυχοι χορεύουσι
τὸν ταμίαν Ἴακχον.

Ἄγγελος
Κάδμου πάροικοι καὶ δόμων Ἀμφίονος,
οὐκ ἔσθ' ὁποῖον στάντ' ἂν ἀνθρώπου βίον
οὔτ' αἰνέσαιμ' ἂν οὔτε μεμψαίμην ποτέ.
τύχη γὰρ ὀρθοῖ καὶ τύχη καταρρέπει
τὸν εὐτυχοῦντα τόν τε δυστυχοῦντ' ἀεί·
καὶ μάντις οὐδεὶς τῶν καθεστώτων βροτοῖς. 1160
Κρέων γὰρ ἦν ζηλωτός, ὡς ἐμοί, ποτέ,
σώσας μὲν ἐχθρῶν τήνδε Καδμείαν χθόνα
λαβών τε χώρας παντελῆ μοναρχίαν
ηὔθυνε, θάλλων εὐγενεῖ τέκνων σπορᾷ·
καὶ νῦν ἀφεῖται πάντα. τὰς γὰρ ἡδονὰς
ὅταν προδῶσιν ἄνδρες, οὐ τίθημ' ἐγὼ
ζῆν τοῦτον, ἀλλ' ἔμψυχον ἡγοῦμαι νεκρόν.
πλούτει τε γὰρ κατ' οἶκον, εἰ βούλει, μέγα
καὶ ζῆ τύραννον σχῆμ' ἔχων· ἐὰν δ' ἀπῇ
τούτων τὸ χαίρειν, τἄλλ' ἐγὼ καπνοῦ σκιᾶς 1170
οὐκ ἂν πριαίμην ἀνδρὶ πρὸς τὴν ἡδονήν.

Χορός
τί δ' αὖ τόδ' ἄχθος βασιλέων ἥκεις φέρων;

Ἄγγελος
τεθνᾶσιν· οἱ δὲ ζῶντες αἴτιοι θανεῖν.

Χορός
καὶ τίς φονεύει; τίς δ' ὁ κείμενος; λέγε.

Ἄγγελος
Αἵμων ὄλωλεν: αὐτόχειρ δ' αἱμάσσεται.

Χορός
πότερα πατρῴας ἢ πρὸς οἰκείας χερός;

Ἄγγελος
αὐτὸς πρὸς αὑτοῦ, πατρὶ μηνίσας φόνου.

Χορός
ὦ μάντι, τοὔπος ὡς ἄρ' ὀρθὸν ἤνυσας.

Ἄγγελος
ὡς ὧδ' ἐχόντων τἄλλα βουλεύειν πάρα.

Χορός
καὶ μὴν ὁρῶ τάλαιναν Εὐρυδίκην ὁμοῦ 1180
δάμαρτα τὴν Κρέοντος. ἐκ δὲ δωμάτων
ἤτοι κλύουσα παιδὸς ἢ τύχῃ πάρα.

Εὐρυδίκη
ὦ πάντες ἀστοί, τῶν λόγων ἐπῃσθόμην
πρὸς ἔξοδον στείχουσα, Παλλάδος θεᾶς
ὅπως ἱκοίμην εὐγμάτων προσήγορος.
καὶ τυγχάνω τε κλῇθρ' ἀνασπαστοῦ πύλης
χαλῶσα καί με φθόγγος οἰκείου κακοῦ
βάλλει δι' ὤτων: ὑπτία δὲ κλίνομαι

δείσασα πρὸς δμωαῖσι κἀποπλήσσομαι
ἀλλ' ὅστις ἦν ὁ μῦθος αὖθις εἴπατε: 1190
κακῶν γὰρ οὐκ ἄπειρος οὐσ' ἀκούσομαι.

Ἄγγελος
ἐγώ, φίλη δέσποινα, καὶ παρὼν ἐρῶ
κοὐδὲν παρήσω τῆς ἀληθείας ἔπος.
τί γάρ σε μαλθάσσοιμ' ἂν ὧν ἐς ὕστερον
ψεῦσται φανούμεθ'; ὀρθὸν ἀλήθει' ἀεί.
ἐγὼ δὲ σῷ ποδαγὸς ἑσπόμην πόσει
πεδίον ἐπ' ἄκρον, ἔνθ' ἔκειτο νηλεὲς
κυνοσπάρακτον σῶμα Πολυνείκους ἔτι·
καὶ τὸν μέν, αἰτήσαντες ἐνοδίαν θεὸν
Πλούτωνά τ' ὀργὰς εὐμενεῖς κατασχεθεῖν 1200
λούσαντες ἁγνὸν λουτρόν, ἐν νεοσπάσιν
θαλλοῖς ὃ δὴ λέλειπτο συγκατῄθομεν,
καὶ τύμβον ὀρθόκρανον οἰκείας χθονὸς
χώσαντες αὖθις πρὸς λιθόστρωτον κόρης
νυμφεῖον Ἅιδου κοῖλον εἰσεβαίνομεν.
φωνῆς δ' ἄπωθεν ὀρθίων κωκυμάτων
κλύει τις ἀκτέριστον ἀμφὶ παστάδα,
καὶ δεσπότῃ Κρέοντι σημαίνει μολών.
τῷ δ' ἀθλίας ἄσημα περιβαίνει βοῆς
ἕρποντι μᾶλλον ἆσσον, οἰμώξας δ' ἔπος 1210
ἵησι δυσθρήνητον· ὦ τάλας ἐγώ,
ἆρ' εἰμὶ μάντις; ἆρα δυστυχεστάτην
κέλευθον ἕρπω τῶν παρελθουσῶν ὁδῶν;
παιδός με σαίνει φθόγγος. ἀλλὰ πρόσπολοι,

Ἀντιγόνη

ἴτ' ἆσσον ὠκεῖς καὶ παραστάντες τάφῳ
ἀθρήσαθ', ἁρμὸν χώματος λιθοσπαδῆ
δύντες πρὸς αὐτὸ στόμιον, εἰ τὸν Αἵμονος
φθόγγον συνίημ' ἢ θεοῖσι κλέπτομαι.
τάδ' ἐξ ἀθύμου δεσπότου κελευσμάτων
ἠθροῦμεν: ἐν δὲ λοισθίῳ τυμβεύματι   1220
τὴν μὲν κρεμαστὴν αὐχένος κατείδομεν,
βρόχῳ μιτώδει σινδόνος καθημμένην,
τὸν δ' ἀμφὶ μέσσῃ περιπετῆ προσκείμενον,
εὐνῆς ἀποιμώζοντα τῆς κάτω φθορὰν
καὶ πατρὸς ἔργα καὶ τὸ δύστηνον λέχος.
ὁ δ' ὡς ὁρᾷ σφε, στυγνὸν οἰμώξας ἔσω
χωρεῖ πρὸς αὐτὸν κἀνακωκύσας καλεῖ:
ὦ τλῆμον, οἷον ἔργον εἴργασαι: τίνα
νοῦν ἔσχες; ἐν τῷ συμφορᾶς διεφθάρης;
ἔξελθε, τέκνον, ἱκέσιός σε λίσσομαι.   1230
τὸν δ' ἀγρίοις ὄσσοισι παπτήνας ὁ παῖς,
πτύσας προσώπῳ κοὐδὲν ἀντειπών, ξίφους
ἕλκει διπλοῦς κνώδοντας. ἐκ δ' ὁρμωμένου
πατρὸς φυγαῖσιν ἤμπλακ': εἶθ' ὁ δύσμορος
αὑτῷ χολωθείς, ὥσπερ εἶχ', ἐπενταθεὶς
ἤρεισε πλευραῖς μέσσον ἔγχος, ἐς δ' ὑγρὸν
ἀγκῶν' ἔτ' ἔμφρων παρθένῳ προσπτύσσεται.
καὶ φυσιῶν ὀξεῖαν ἐκβάλλει ῥοὴν
λευκῇ παρειᾷ φοινίου σταλάγματος.
κεῖται δὲ νεκρὸς περὶ νεκρῷ, τὰ νυμφικὰ   1240
τέλη λαχὼν δείλαιος εἰν Ἅιδου δόμοις,
δείξας ἐν ἀνθρώποισι τὴν ἀβουλίαν

ὅσῳ μέγιστον ἀνδρὶ πρόσκειται κακόν.

Χορός
τί τοῦτ' ἂν εἰκάσειας; ἡ γυνὴ πάλιν
φρούδη, πρὶν εἰπεῖν ἐσθλὸν ἢ κακὸν λόγον.

Ἄγγελος
καὐτὸς τεθάμβηκ': ἐλπίσιν δὲ βόσκομαι
ἄχη τέκνου κλύουσαν ἐς πόλιν γόους
οὐκ ἀξιώσειν, ἀλλ' ὑπὸ στέγης ἔσω
δμωαῖς προθήσειν πένθος οἰκεῖον στένειν.
γνώμης γὰρ οὐκ ἄπειρος, ὥσθ' ἁμαρτάνειν. 1250

Χορός
οὐκ οἶδ': ἐμοὶ δ' οὖν ἥ τ' ἄγαν σιγὴ βαρὺ
δοκεῖ προσεῖναι χἠ μάτην πολλὴ βοή.

Ἄγγελος
ἀλλ' εἰσόμεσθα, μή τι καὶ κατάσχετον
κρυφῇ καλύπτει καρδίᾳ θυμουμένῃ,
δόμους παραστείχοντες: εὖ γὰρ οὖν λέγεις,
καὶ τῆς ἄγαν γάρ ἐστί που σιγῆς βάρος.

Χορός
καὶ μὴν ὅδ' ἄναξ αὐτὸς ἐφήκει
μνῆμ' ἐπίσημον διὰ χειρὸς ἔχων,
εἰ θέμις εἰπεῖν, οὐκ ἀλλοτρίαν
ἄτην, ἀλλ' αὐτὸς ἁμαρτών. 1260

Κρέων
ἰὼ
φρενῶν δυσφρόνων ἁμαρτήματα
στερεὰ θανατόεντ',
ὦ κτανόντας τε καὶ
θανόντας βλέποντες ἐμφυλίους.
ὤμοι ἐμῶν ἄνολβα βουλευμάτων.
ἰὼ παῖ, νέος νέῳ ξὺν μόρῳ
αἰαῖ αἰαῖ,
ἔθανες, ἀπελύθης
ἐμαῖς οὐδὲ σαῖς δυσβουλίαις.

Χορός
οἴμ' ὡς ἔοικας ὀψὲ τὴν δίκην ἰδεῖν. 1270

Κρέων
οἴμοι, ἔχω μαθὼν δείλαιος· ἐν δ' ἐμῷ κάρᾳ
θεὸς τότ' ἄρα τότε μέγα βάρος μ' ἔχων
ἔπαισεν, ἐν δ' ἔσεισεν ἀγρίαις ὁδοῖς,
οἴμοι, λακπάτητον ἀντρέπων χαράν.
φεῦ φεῦ, ὦ πόνοι βροτῶν δύσπονοι.

Ἐξάγγελος
Ὦ δέσποθ', ὡς ἔχων τε καὶ κεκτημένος,
τὰ μὲν πρὸ χειρῶν τάδε φέρων, τὰ δ' ἐν δόμοις
ἔοικας ἥκων καὶ τάχ' ὄψεσθαι κακά. 1280

Κρέων
τί δ' ἔστιν αὖ κάκιον ἐκ κακῶν ἔτι;

Ἐξάγγελος
γυνὴ τέθνηκε, τοῦδε παμμήτωρ νεκροῦ,
δύστηνος, ἄρτι νεοτόμοισι πλήγμασιν.

Κρέων
ἰώ. ἰὼ δυσκάθαρτος Ἅιδου λιμήν,
τί μ' ἄρα τί μ' ὀλέκεις;
ὦ κακάγγελτά μοι
προπέμψας ἄχη, τίνα θροεῖς λόγον;
αἰαῖ, ὀλωλότ' ἄνδρ' ἐπεξειργάσω.
τί φής, παῖ; τίν' αὖ λέγεις μοι νέον, 1290
αἰαῖ αἰαῖ,
σφάγιον ἐπ' ὀλέθρῳ
γυναικεῖον ἀμφικεῖσθαι μόρον;

Χορός
ὁρᾶν πάρεστιν: οὐ γὰρ ἐν μυχοῖς ἔτι.

Κρέων
Οἴμοι,
κακὸν τόδ' ἄλλο δεύτερον βλέπω τάλας
Τίς ἄρα, τίς με πότμος ἔτι περιμένει;
Ἔχω μὲν ἐν χείρεσσιν ἀρτίως τέκνον,
τάλας, τὸν δ' ἔναντα προσβλέπω νεκρόν. 1300
Φεῦ φεῦ μᾶτερ ἀθλία, φεῦ τέκνον.

Ἐξάγγελος
Ἡ δ' ὀξύπληκτος ἠμένη δὲ βωμία
λύει κελαινὰ βλέφαρα, κωκύσασα μὲν
τοῦ πρὶν θανόντος Μεγαρέως κλεινὸν λάχος,
αὖθις δὲ τοῦδε, λοίσθιον δὲ σοὶ κακὰς
πράξεις ἐφυμνήσασα τῷ παιδοκτόνῳ.

Κρέων
αἰαῖ αἰαῖ,
ἀνέπταν φόβῳ. τί μ' οὐκ ἀνταίαν
ἔπαισέν τις ἀμφιθήκτῳ ξίφει;
δείλαιος ἐγώ, αἰαῖ, 1310
δειλαίᾳ δὲ συγκέκραμαι δύᾳ.

Ἐξάγγελος
ὡς αἰτίαν γε τῶνδε κἀκείνων ἔχων
πρὸς τῆς θανούσης τῆσδ' ἐπεσκήπτου μόρων

Κρέων
ποίῳ δὲ κἀπελύσατ' ἐν φοναῖς τρόπῳ;

Ἐξάγγελος
παίσας ὑφ' ἧπαρ αὐτόχειρ αὑτήν, ὅπως
παιδὸς τόδ' ᾔσθετ' ὀξυκώκυτον πάθος.

Κρέων
ὤμοι μοι, τάδ' οὐκ ἐπ' ἄλλον βροτῶν
ἐμᾶς ἁρμόσει ποτ' ἐξ αἰτίας.
ἐγὼ γάρ σ' ἐγὼ ἔκανον, ὦ μέλεος,
ἐγώ, φάμ' ἔτυμον. ἰὼ πρόσπολοι, 1320
ἄγετέ μ' ὅτι τάχιστ', ἄγετέ μ' ἐκποδών,
τὸν οὐκ ὄντα μᾶλλον ἢ μηδένα.

Χορός
κέρδη παραινεῖς, εἴ τι κέρδος ἐν κακοῖς.
βράχιστα γὰρ κράτιστα τἀν ποσὶν κακά.

Κρέων
ἴτω ἴτω,
φανήτω μόρων ὁ κάλλιστ' ἔχων
ἐμοὶ τερμίαν ἄγων ἁμέραν 1330
ὕπατος· ἴτω ἴτω,
ὅπως μηκέτ' ἆμαρ ἄλλ' εἰσίδω.

Χορός
μέλλοντα ταῦτα. τῶν προκειμένων τι χρὴ μέλειν
πράσσειν. μέλει γὰρ τῶνδ' ὅτοισι χρὴ μέλειν

Κρέων
ἀλλ' ὧν ἐρῶ, τοιαῦτα συγκατηυξάμην.

Χορός
μή νυν προσεύχου μηδέν· ὡς πεπρωμένης
οὐκ ἔστι θνητοῖς συμφορᾶς ἀπαλλαγή.

Κρέων
ἄγοιτ' ἂν μάταιον ἄνδρ' ἐκποδών,
ὅς, ὦ παῖ, σέ τ' οὐχ ἑκὼν κάκτανον   1340
σέ τ' αὖ τάνδ', ὤμοι μέλεος, οὐδ' ἔχω
ὅπᾳ πρὸς πότερα κλιθῶ· πάντα γὰρ
λέχρια τἀν χεροῖν, τὰ δ' ἐπὶ κρατί μοι
πότμος δυσκόμιστος εἰσήλατο.

Χορός
πολλῷ τὸ φρονεῖν εὐδαιμονίας
πρῶτον ὑπάρχει. χρὴ δὲ τά γ' εἰς θεοὺς
μηδὲν ἀσεπτεῖν. μεγάλοι δὲ λόγοι   1350
μεγάλας πληγὰς τῶν ὑπεραύχων
ἀποτίσαντες
γήρᾳ τὸ φρονεῖν ἐδίδαξαν.

GENEALOGY OF
THE ROYAL HOUSE OF THEBES

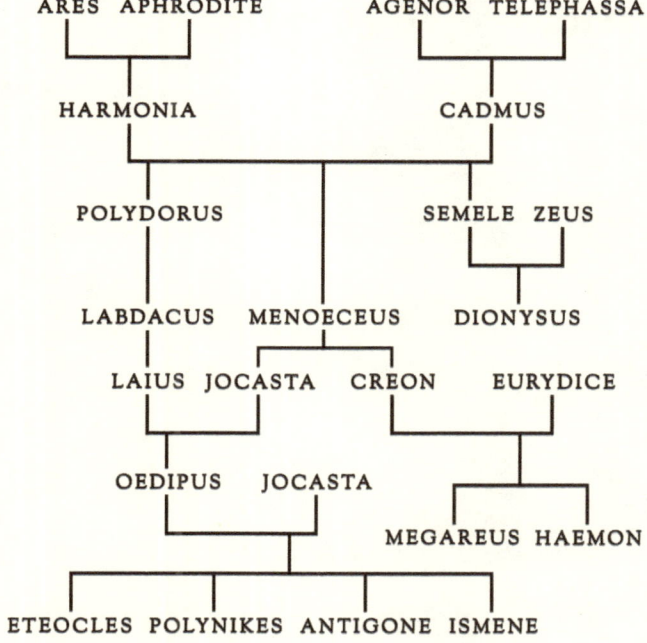

GLOSSARY

ACHERON (Ἀχέρων) One of the five rivers of the underworld, named for the god who was said to have been transformed into the river. Sometimes referred to as the "river of woe", it was across these waters that Charon ferried the souls of the dead into Hades.

AMPHION (Ἀμφίων) One of the founding kings of Thebes, who is said to have taken Niobe, daughter of Tantalus, as his wife.

APHRODITE (Αφροδιτη) Goddess of love and beauty.

ARES (Αρης) God of war and battle-lust.

ARGOS (Αργος) A powerful city in the northeastern portion of the Peloponnese.

ARTEMIS (Αρτεμις) Virgin goddess of the hunt, wilderness, and the sublime in nature.

ATHENA (Αθηνη) Goddess of wisdom and good counsel. She was the patron deity of Athens and played an important role in the maintenance of law and justice.

BACCHUS (Βάκχος) Another name for Dionysus

BOREAS (Βορεας) Winged God of the north-wind and winter.

CADMUS (Κάδμος) Legendary founder of Thebes and foremost among the great heroes of ancient times. At the spring of Ismene, Cadmus slew a dragon and, as instructed by Athena, planted the monster's teeth in the soil. From the ground there sprang a race of fierce warriors, the *Spartoi* ("sown"), from whom the noble families of Thebes descend.

CASTALIA (Κασταλια) A sacred spring at Delphi.

CITHÆRON (Κιθαιρών) A mountain range between Corinth and Thebes.

CLEOPATRA (Κλεοπάτρα) Daughter of the wind-god, Boreas, and the Athenian princess, Orithyia; granddaughter of Erechtheus.

CORYCIÆ (Κωρυκιαι) Nymphs associated with the Corycian Caves, a sacred site upon Mount Parnassus pre-dating the Bronze Age.

DANAË (Δανάη) An Argive princess who was shut away by her father, King Acrisius, after the Delphic oracle informed him that he would have no male heir, but that his daughter would bear a son who was fated to kill him. Zeus impregnated Danaë through a shower of golden rain while she was confined and thus she gave birth to the hero Perseus.

DELPHI (Δελφοί) A sacred precinct in ancient Greece that was home to the famous oracle of Apollo, who was believed to be able to communicate with the god of truth, reason, and prophecy. The Delphic oracle was consulted by people throughout the ancient world on matters of great importance, such as war, laws, and the founding of new cities.

DEMETER (Δημητηρ) Goddess of the harvest and agriculture, at times associated with the underworld, specifically her role in the Mystery Cults which offered its initiates the chance of reaching Elysium after death.

DIONYSUS (Διονυσος) God of wine and festivity. His worship was historically associated with revelry and divine frenzy, though over time took on various different forms including the esoteric mystery cults.

DIRCE (Δίρκη) A Naiad (water nymph) whose spring near Thebes was sacred to the god Dionysus.

EDONIA (Ἡδωνίδα) An ancient city in southern Thrace.

ELEUSIS (Ελευσις) An ancient town in Attica renowned for its worship of Demeter and the local mystery cult, the Eleusinian Mysteries.

EREBUS (Ερεβος) Primordial god of darkness. The term "Erebus" was used variously to refer to the underworld itself, a portion of the underworld, or the space between Hades and Earth.

ERECHTHEUS (Ἐρεχθεύς) A legendary king of Athens who came to be divinised in the city-state. Athenians referred to themselves as "Erechtheidai", or "sons of Erechtheus".

ERINYES (Ερινυες) Three winged goddesses of vengeance who punished men for their crimes against divine law. As agents of retributive justice, they were often invoked by a victim as a curse upon their offender. As most famously seen in Aeschylus' *Oresteia*, the most powerful of these curses came from a parent who had been wronged by their child.

EROS (Ερως) God of love, usually considered to be the son of Aphrodite. He also represented desire, particularly in poetry, both in the sense of affection between people as well as the urge which drives men to act, or which can consume them in their endeavours.

FURIES Another name for the Erinyes

HADES (Αιδης) God of death and king of the underworld. The House of Hades, or simply Hades, referred to the land of the dead, populated by the spirits, or shades, of the deceased.

HECATE (Εκατη) Goddess of entrance-ways, crossroads, graves, spirits of the dead, night-time, and light, often depicted holding twin torches.

HEPHAESTUS (Ηφαιστος) God of fire, craftsmanship, and metalworking.

ISMENUS (Ἰσμηνος) Bœotian river-god. His stream flowed from the western foothills of Mount Cithæron down past the city of Thebes.

JUSTICE Dike (Δικη) was the goddess of justice, fair judgement, and the upholding of divine law. She was invoked to both defend the just and punish the unjust. Her mother, Themis, was also a goddess of justice.

LACEDÆMON (Λακεδαίμων) The mythical king of Laconia. His name was used in antiquity to refer to Sparta.

LYCURGUS (Λυκοῦργος) King of the Edoni, in Thrace. He was driven mad by Dionysus after persecuting the god's followers, the Mænads.

NIOBE (Νιόβη) Daughter of the Phrygian king Tantalus, and, according to some accounts, wife of Amphion. During an annual celebration in honour of the goddess Leto, mother of Apollo and Artemis, Niobe made a blasphemous boast that she was more worthy of worship as she had fourteen children. Enraged, Leto had Apollo and Artemis kill all of her children. Niobe then fled back to Mount Sipylus where she was turned to stone while weeping in her devastation.

OLYMPUS (Ὀλυμπος) The abode of the heavenly gods. Described as a fortified complex of gold and marble palaces which stood upon the peaks of Mount Olympus in northern Greece.

PARNASSUS (Παρνασσός) A mountain range in central Greece which was considered sacred to both Dionysus and Apollo. It was also thought to be the home of the Muses.

PHRYGIA (Φρυγία) An ancient kingdom situated in western Anatolia.

POLIS (πόλις) A city, or city-state. The term could also be used to refer to a community, the wider nation, or the state itself.

POSEIDON (Ποσειδων) God of the sea and earthquakes.

PLUTO (Πλούτων) Another name for the god of the underworld.

SALMYDESSUS (Σαλμυδησσός) Ancient town on the northern coast of Thrace, just west of the entrance to the Bosphorus Strait.

SARDIS (Σάρδεις) Ancient city and capital of the Lydian Empire, situated in western Anatolia.

SEMELE (Σεμελη) A Theban princess and mother of Dionysus.

THEBES (Θῆβαι) One of Ancient Greece's foremost cities, situated on the Bœotian plain, to the northwest of Athens.

THRACE (Θράκη) A historical region to the northeast of Greece, bordering the Ægean and Black seas.

ZEUS HOMAIMOS (Ζεὺς σύναιμος) Zeus as protector of familial ties and the sanctity of blood kinship.

OTHER TITLES FROM INVICTUS PUBLISHING

On Rome and the Gods: The Life and Works of Emperor Julian
Edward Alexander

Flavius Claudius Julianus, better known to history as "Julian the Apostate", was the last Pagan Emperor to ever rule Rome. Despite his formally Christian upbringing, the nephew of Constantine the Great was irrepressibly drawn from a young age to the gods of old. With Christianity coming to predominate among the Roman elite, and Pagan religions throughout the Empire struggling to endure in the face of restrictive laws and violent coercion, Julian sought to protect, unify, and revitalise the ailing Greco-Roman faith during his tragically brief rule.

As a keen student of philosophy, Julian wrote prodigiously on a wide range of subjects including Neo-Platonism, Greco-Roman theology, just rulership, mythology, and the religious struggle between Christianity and traditional polytheism. All fourteen of Julian's extant works and an extensive collection of letters are reproduced here with an improved translation by Edward Alexander, along with an original biography of the fourth century Emperor.

OTHER TITLES FROM INVICTUS PUBLISHING

Polybius and the Roman Conquest of Greece: How Hellenic Disunity Gave Rise to Roman Rule

Fustel de Coulanges

Less than two centuries after the death of Alexander the Great, Greece had been reduced to a province of the nascent Roman empire. In Polybius and the Roman Conquest of Greece, Fustel de Coulanges explores the key social and political conditions which led to Greece's subjugation, from the fierce divisions that had long plagued Ancient Greek society, to the unassailable disunity between the Hellenic city-states. Uncompromising in his analysis, Coulanges details the fractured resistance to Roman conquest through the lens of Polybius' writings, exploring how "the last historian of a free Greece" would ultimately come to view Rome as the solution to the deep disorders of his homeland.

OTHER TITLES FROM INVICTUS PUBLISHING

The Samurai: History, Bushidō, and the Way of the Sword
William Ashcroft

William Ashcroft's "The Samurai" traces the long and storied history of Japan's famous warrior class, detailing the great battles, legendary figures, and key developments that shaped the samurai over the centuries, together with an exploration of bushidō – the Way of the Warrior – and the art of swordsmanship, drawing on works by Yamamoto Jōchō and Miyamoto Musashi.

Ashcroft's concise history expertly charts the emergence of the samurai during the early imperial age, their rise to national dominance, and their eventual dissolution upon the founding of the modern Japanese state. Traversing over a thousand years of history, The Samurai covers such subjects as seppuku, the daring feats of Minamoto no Yoshitsune, the last stand of Kusunoki Masashige, the tumultuous Sengoku Jidai ("Age of the Country at War"), the famed vendetta of the forty-seven rōnin, and the Satsuma Rebellion – the last samurai uprising and the last civil war in Japanese history.

www.ingramcontent.com/pod-product-compliance
Lightning Source LLC
Chambersburg PA
CBHW030434010526
44118CB00011B/625